Topz GOSPELS

LUKE

ALEXA TEWKESBURY

CWR

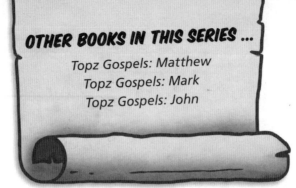

OTHER BOOKS IN THIS SERIES ...

Topz Gospels: Matthew
Topz Gospels: Mark
Topz Gospels: John

Copyright © CWR 2015
Published 2015 by CWR, Waverley Abbey House, Waverley Lane, Farnham, Surrey GU9 8EP, UK. Registered Charity No. 294387. Registered Limited Company No. 1990308.

The right of Alexa Tewkesbury to be identified as the author of this work has been asserted by her in accordance with the Copyright, Designs and Patents Act 1988, sections 77 and 78.

For a list of National Distributors visit www.cwr.org.uk/distributors

All Scripture references are from the Good News Bible (Anglicised), copyright © American Bible Society 1966, 1971, 1976, 1992, 1994, 2004.

Concept development, editing, design and production by CWR
Cover Illustrations: Mike Henson at CWR
Internal Illustrations: Ben Knight at CWR
Printed in the UK by Page Bros
ISBN: 978-1-78259-400-0

Introduction by Josie

Do you ever read a book and find you love it SO much that the story just bursts into life right off the page? You can *see* the people; *hear* them talk to each other as if they're talking to you; *feel* everything they feel.

The words turn into something so real that it could be *you* in the story.

It could be *your* adventure.

That's what happened when I started to read Luke's Gospel in the Bible. I felt as if I was there!

The chapters are full of what Jesus did and what Jesus taught. Jesus speaks about praying to God and trusting Him; about God's love and forgiveness. Luke has written down stories that Jesus told, too.

Stories that help us understand what Jesus wants us to know and to remember.

And it feels so real.

I know I wasn't there. If I had been I'd be so old and shrivelled now, I probably wouldn't even look like a person!

But when I read Luke's Gospel, it feels as though I *could* have been there!

Topz and me and Jesus.

And if I *could* have been there, maybe this is what it would have been like ...

CHAPTER 1
The Woman and the Jar
(Luke 7:36–37)

Josie waves. 'Sarah!'

Sarah stops walking. She looks around. There's no one there. No one for as far as she can see.

'Sarah!'

'That's Josie again, Saucy,' Sarah says to the little cat nestled in her arms. 'But where is she?'

She hears Josie start to laugh. From somewhere. She frowns.

'I can hear you but I can't see you,' she calls. 'Come on, Josie, where are you?'

Josie still laughs. 'Look up,' she giggles.

Sarah tilts her head. 'Up? Up where?'

'Straight ahead and up.'

Three trees stand a short way off in front of Sarah. Leaves cling thickly to the broad ladders of their branches.

Sarah squints past them. Beyond them, there is nothing. Just the track that leads away from the nearby town and on across the dry and dusty plains. There's no Josie.

Sarah's getting impatient. 'I'm looking and I still can't see you. Where are you?' She blinks into the distance. 'Why don't you just come here? Saucy, where is she?'

Saucy closes her eyes and dozes. She's warm and comfy in Sarah's arms and she doesn't really care where anyone is.

Josie calls again: 'I'm here, Sarah.'

Sarah sighs. Once more, she peers ahead of her and upwards.

This time, her eye is caught by something. Movement – a couple of branches up among the leaves of the middle tree. A hand waves. A face peeps out. There's another burst of giggles and Sarah spies Josie's impish grin.

'Ha! How did you get up there?'

'How d'you think?' laughs Josie. 'I climbed! Come on up.'

'No.' Sarah shakes her head. 'I'm no good at climbing trees. Anyway, I can't. I've got Saucy.'

'Put her in your bag,' says Josie. 'In fact, Saucy could climb up by herself. Put her down and I'll call her.'

Again, 'No,' Sarah says. 'Not now, she's asleep. You know she hates me waking her up when she's asleep.'

'Oh, *please*! You'll love it once you're up here. You can see for miles.'

Sarah presses her lips together. Once more she shakes her head.

Josie gives up. 'You *are* funny! I'm not even up very high. Hang on, then. I'll come down.'

Her face disappears. Leaves shiver and rustle as she slips carefully down from her hiding place. Her feet reach the branch underneath. From there it's only a short drop to the ground.

Josie lands lightly – easily. She gives Sarah a wave and goes to step towards her.

THAT'S WHEN SHE SEES JESUS.

Sarah spots Him, too.

He passes close to them as He walks along with another man. The two of them talk. They seem so deep in their conversation that they don't notice the Topz girls.

'Weird,' whispers Josie.

'Why weird?' Sarah glances at her.

'That man with Jesus.' Josie nods towards him. 'I think he's called Simon.'

'So?' Sarah shrugs.

'So,' says Josie, 'he's a Pharisee. He's one of those teachers of the Law. They don't talk about God's love and forgiveness the way Jesus does. They just talk about rules. About what you mustn't do and when you mustn't do it – or what you *must* do and when you *must* do it. They don't understand who God really is. And worse than that,' she adds, 'they *hate* Jesus for the way He talks and the things He does.'

Sarah watches the two men as they walk away – as they head towards the town.

'That man doesn't look as if he hates Jesus,' she says. 'He looks as if he's really listening to Him. Really properly listening to Him.'

'I know,' nods Josie. 'That's why it's weird.'

They both stare after the men for another moment.

They throw each other a glance and then, without a word, follow behind them towards the town.

Outside Simon's house, the two men stop. Simon ushers Jesus inside.

'Look at that!' whispers Josie. 'Simon's invited Him in. He's actually invited Jesus into his house!'

Other people have noticed Simon walk with Jesus through the town's streets. Other people see them step into Simon's house together.

So, before long, the news spreads. **NEWS OF JESUS ALWAYS SPREADS.** Even when He asks people to keep quiet about the good things He's done for them, they never can. And on this particular day, in this particular town, the news spreads to the ears of a woman who lives there.

'What?' she murmurs to herself. 'Am I hearing right?'

There's so much excitement, it's impossible for her not to hear something. And what she hears is that Jesus is having dinner with Simon, the Pharisee.

This woman is unhappy. She does things that she knows are wrong. The people of the town are not perfect people. Still, they look down their noses at her. They won't have anything to do with her. Instead, they whisper about her. They see her walking towards them and they cross over to the other side of the street.

But Jesus speaks about God's love and about how to be God's friend. Jesus teaches that God forgives people who are truly sorry for the wrong things they do.

With God, Jesus says, everyone can have a brand-new life to live.

And as soon as the woman knows Jesus is there, she can't keep away from Him. She stops what she's doing and runs through the streets towards Simon's house.

Standing on the opposite side of the road, Sarah sees her. She nudges Josie; nods her head towards the figure who now stands, uncertain and out of breath, outside the front door. **IN HER HANDS SHE HOLDS A STONE JAR.**

There are people staring at her, she knows that. People who must wonder how she dares to stand at the door of a Pharisee. How she dares to show her face at all.

But she ignores them. She has to ignore them.

To do what she needs to do she must step through the doorway to meet Jesus. No matter how people stare at her – or what they think.

CHAPTER 2
A Brand-New Life
(Luke 7:37–50)

It's late in the day but still the sun beams down.
The woman at Simon's door takes a deep breath. She slips
through it into the house and into the shadows. As Josie
and Sarah watch from the brightness of the street, she
seems to become a shadow herself.

Close behind them, someone complains, 'What does
that woman think she's doing? Shoving her way into
Simon's house like that without being invited!'

'She wouldn't last five minutes in *my* house,'
another voice replies. 'A woman like that? Simon'll
throw her out in a moment, you wait and see!'

Inside the house, Jesus and Simon sit at a table near
the front door. Some of Simon's friends have been
invited, too, and they sit with them.

As the woman steps in from the street, it's Simon
who sees her first. He falls silent. He scowls.

HOW DARE SHE?

Simon watches as she moves to stand behind Jesus.
Just behind Him.

She takes in another breath and drops onto her

knees at His feet. Jesus is here! Right in front of her! Jesus who loves people and makes them well and speaks about forgiveness.

Jesus, the way to God!

If the woman put out a hand, she could touch Him. He's so close – they breathe the same air.

And suddenly there are tears in her eyes. Her sobs are silent but the tears stream down her face. They drop to the floor. They fall, one after the other, onto Jesus' sandalled feet. Still crying, she pulls her long hair over one shoulder and uses it to wipe the tears away. Then she leans forward and kisses His feet.

Simon's mouth twists spitefully. His eyes dart from the woman to Jesus in disbelief. They stretch even wider as he watches what she does next.

She picks up the stone jar she has brought with her and opens it. There is perfume inside. Very expensive perfume. The moment it is uncovered, the scent fills the air. It's powerful but beautiful. It drifts through the open doorway. Sarah and Josie notice it in the street.

Then carefully, lovingly, the woman tilts the jar and, little by little, the perfume trickles out. She pours until Jesus' feet are bathed in the sweet smell. She pours until the jar is empty.

Simon is horrified. It's not just that this woman is touching Jesus – it's that Jesus doesn't seem to mind!

Tutting with disgust, the Pharisee can't keep his thoughts to himself.

'Well, here's a fine thing,' he mutters. 'If this Man is really the Prophet people say He is, He'd put a stop to this. He'd know exactly who this woman is and the sort of life she lives. He'd know of every bad thing she has ever done!'

Jesus looks at him; stares into him. 'Simon, there's something I want to say to you.'

'Of course,' Simon answers. 'Say it, speak to me.'

'A moneylender was owed some money by two men,' Jesus begins. 'One man owed five hundred silver coins, while the other owed fifty silver coins. Neither of the men were able to pay back the money. So the moneylender said, "That's all right. I'll cancel both your debts. Now neither of you owe me anything."'

Jesus stops speaking. He gazes down at the woman who still kneels at His feet.

He asks, 'Tell me, Simon – which one of those two men will love the moneylender more?'

Simon watches Jesus. He looks thoughtful as he considers the question.

'Well,' he answers finally, 'I suppose it would be the man who owed five hundred silver coins. When the moneylender cancelled the two debts, the man who owed more was forgiven more. So – he's bound to love the moneylender more for his kindness.'

Jesus nods. 'That's right,' He says.

Once again, He looks at the woman who has searched Him out; who has found Him in Simon's house.

He asks, 'You see this woman, Simon? When I walked into your house, you didn't provide me with any water to wash my feet. But this woman has washed them in her tears, and she has wiped them dry with her hair. And I didn't notice you welcome me with a kiss. But this woman – she has hardly stopped kissing my feet since she came in.'

Jesus pauses. He stares again deep into Simon.

'You gave no olive oil for my head, Simon. Did you? This woman, though – this woman has poured expensive perfume all over my feet. Don't you see? This woman knows that there is a lot wrong with the life she lives. She knows she has done many wrong things. But she also knows that she needs God to forgive her.'

He smiles down at the woman. His eyes glow with such kindness.

'What this woman has done for me today, Simon,' He continues, 'the love she has shown me – it's huge! It proves how much she *knows* she needs forgiveness and how much God has forgiven her.

'You see, someone who doesn't think there is anything wrong with the way they live their life – someone who doesn't feel they need God to forgive them for very much at all – that person doesn't do something as big as this. That person thinks all they need to show is just a *little* bit of love.'

Simon says nothing. He just clamps his jaws tightly together and watches his guest in silence as Jesus speaks to the woman for the first time:

'It's all right now. All those wrong things you've done? They are forgiven.'

Still Simon doesn't say a word. But the friends at his supper table can't keep quiet. They start to nudge each other and murmur.

'Who is this Man?'

'How's this possible?'

'Did you hear what He said? Seriously, how can He forgive sins?'

Jesus takes no notice. He simply smiles again at the woman at His feet. A warm, wonderful smile.

'**YOUR TRUST IN ME HAS SET YOU FREE** to live a brand-new, clean life,' He says. 'Go now. Be happy.'

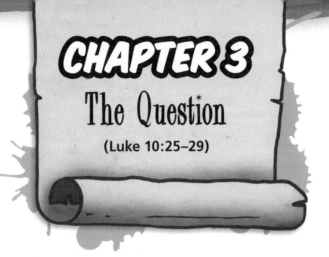

CHAPTER 3
The Question*
(Luke 10:25–29)

Danny and Benny stretch out on the dry ground at the top of the hill, and roll. Downwards.

The slope is steep.

They flip over and over. The sharp angle of the hillside turns them faster and faster. They can't stop even if they want to.

Benny *does* want to.

'Help!' he yelps. 'I need to stop! Now! Help!'

As the slope shallows, the spinning of his body finally slows with the flatter ground and he groans to a halt. But the spinning inside his head continues.

'That was horrible,' he moans. 'That's the worst thing I've ever done … Ever … Seriously, in my whole life ever!'

Danny springs to his feet. 'What are you talking about?' he grins. 'That was the *coolest* thing *I've* ever done in my whole life ever!'

Benny grunts. 'That's 'cos you're a weirdo.' He doesn't open his eyes. He squeezes them tight shut and presses the heels of his hands into them.

'I want to do it again,' says Danny.

'I just want everything to stop going round,' whimpers Benny.

'Come on, open your eyes.'

'No ...'

'Open them!'

'No!'

Danny shrugs and gives up. He glances towards the brow of the hill. The rest of the Topz Gang stand there in a row and look down at the two boys.

'Who else wants to give it a go?' he calls.

'Erm ... not sure,' Paul calls back. Then, 'How bad is it, Benny?'

'It's bad!' wails Benny. 'Stonkingly bad. And even worse than that! This is not something you want to do. Not ever. Trust me.'

Paul glances at his friends. They look at each other; all nod together.

'That's good enough for us,' says Paul. 'I think we'll give it a miss, Danny.'

Danny looks disappointed. 'You know your trouble, don't you?' he says. 'No sense of adventure.'

'And you know yours, don't you?' mumbles Benny. 'No sense!'

At last, he takes his hands gingerly from his eyes, but still doesn't open them. Carefully, he pushes himself upright until he sits hunched on the ground.

Danny is already making his way back up to the hilltop to take a second roll down. Solo this time.

'Anyone got any water?' Benny whimpers. 'I think I need water.'

Topz shake their heads.

'We'll find some in the next village,' says Josie.

'And some food, I hope,' says Dave. 'I'm starving!'

'Don't mention food!' howls Benny. 'I couldn't eat – I honestly couldn't.'

'Whoa, serious!' laughs Sarah.

As Danny rolls, the other Topz make their way, on foot, down the hill.

'Ready, Benny?' calls John.

'Do I look ready?' Benny mutters.

John shrugs. 'See you there, then.'

Benny opens his eyes, blinks several times and drags himself to his feet.

'That's it, you go on,' he grumbles. 'Don't worry about me, I'll be fine. Completely fine. Stonkingly, fandabulously fine ...'

As they near the village, Topz see a group of men up ahead of them. Josie spots Peter first; then Jesus, who stands a little apart from the others and talks to them. The men are all His disciples.

'Wait,' Josie says. Her eyes light up. 'D'you see Him? Jesus? Let's wait a minute.'

Topz stop where they are. They don't want to interrupt. They know Jesus is well used to interruptions, but they stop walking even so. A tree stands at the edge of the track and they sit down under it. In the shade. Out of the hot sun.

But as they watch, another man heads towards Jesus from the direction of the village.

'Teacher!' he calls. 'Teacher!' He waves to attract Jesus' attention.

So Jesus is interrupted after all.

He finishes what He is saying and turns towards the intruder.

'Please tell me something, Teacher,' the man says. 'You talk about eternal life. Life with God forever. So tell me, what must I do to receive that eternal life?'

Josie smiles.

'It's about love,' she murmurs. 'That's what Jesus will say. Everything to do with God is about love. Love is what God is.'

John shakes his head. 'I don't think that man wants to know about God's love.'

Sarah glances at him. 'Of course he does, why wouldn't he?'

'I've seen him before,' John answers. 'He's one of those teachers of the Law. They don't like what Jesus says. All they care about is keeping rules. That man's not interested in God's love. I think he's just trying to catch Jesus out.'

Jesus studies the man a moment. He knows perfectly well who he is. He doesn't answer him. Not straightaway.

Instead, 'You read what it says in the Scriptures, don't you?' He asks. 'What do they tell you to do? What do you think they mean?'

The man draws his brows together. 'Well,' he says, 'the Scriptures tell us to love the Lord our God with our whole hearts. To love Him with every part of us, deep inside our souls. To love Him with all the energy and enthusiasm that we possibly can, and with every thought in our heads.'

The man stops speaking. He searches Jesus' face, peers at Him with keen, sharp eyes. He knows he is right, but how will Jesus answer?

Jesus says nothing, as if He's waiting for something else.

'And,' the man continues, 'the Scriptures also say that we are to love our neighbours as we love ourselves.'

This time, Jesus smiles and nods His head. 'Good,' He replies. 'That's exactly right. Do those things – love God and your neighbour just as the Scriptures tell you. That's how to live with God forever.'

Josie's eyes shine. 'You see?' she whispers. 'God is all about love. And we can have life with Him forever because of that love.'

Jesus goes to turn back to His disciples, but the man hasn't finished. He has another question.

'Yes, but, Teacher,' he begins again, 'who is my "neighbour"?'

This time there is a strange glint in the man's eye.

A LOOK OF SMUGNESS ON HIS FACE.

'God might be all about love, but that man isn't,' John mutters. 'I don't think he cares about love one bit.'

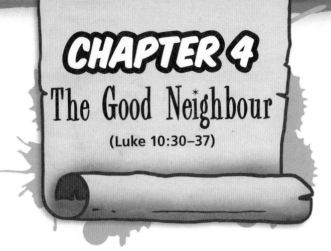

CHAPTER 4
The Good Neighbour
(Luke 10:30–37)

Jesus looks curiously at the man in front of Him.
He explores his face through the deep pools of His eyes.
They uncover what's in the man's heart – the thoughts
that are inside his head.

Jesus sees right through him.

'Who is your neighbour?' He says thoughtfully.
Then, 'Let me tell you a story. A Jewish man was
making a journey on foot from the city of Jerusalem
to Jericho. As he walked along, head down, minding
his own business, he was attacked by a gang of
robbers. They knocked him to the ground and took his
clothes and everything else he had with him. As if that
wasn't enough, they then beat him till he looked more
dead than alive. And when they had finished with
him, they ran off.'

Sitting under the tree beside the road, Topz are close
enough to hear every word.

Benny frowns. 'I thought this story was going to
be about love,' he mutters. 'Doesn't sound very
loving to me.'

'This was a lonely place,' Jesus continues. 'A dangerous place. Not many people went that way. The man who lay bleeding in the dirt desperately needed help but *who* was there to help him ...?

'Wait – there was someone. As it happened, a priest was walking quickly along that same piece of road. He slowed down when he spotted the man lying there. He stopped when he noticed his horrible injuries. He could see how much the man needed someone to help him.

'But, what did the priest do?' Jesus asks. 'He crossed over to the other side of the road and hurried on past.'

Benny shakes his head. He's confused. 'Hang on, that's a *priest* Jesus is talking about. How can he just walk away? What sort of a story is this?'

'So,' Jesus goes on, 'the wounded man still lay there on the ground in that dangerous place. That very lonely place. And things looked bad for him. What were the chances of anyone else travelling that way?

'But then, someone else did. Like the priest, this second person also worked in the Temple. Surely he would rush over to the injured man and do whatever he could for him. Wouldn't he ...?'

'Well, yeah, he must,' Benny thinks. 'He must. He's got to.'

'No,' says Jesus. His attention is still fixed on the man in front of Him, but it's as if He reads Benny's thoughts. 'As it turned out he wouldn't lift a finger to help. Just like the priest before him, he took one look at the man, crossed the road like a shot and couldn't get away from him fast enough.

22

'So – what hope was there for the poor wounded victim now? If men who worked for God wouldn't help him, who was there to save him?'

The teacher of the Law eyes Jesus carefully, but says nothing.

'Well, it just so happened,' Jesus says, 'that a man from Samaria was also making a journey along that stretch of road, with his donkey.'

'Well, *he* won't help,' whispers Dave. 'The man who's hurt is a Jew, and Samaritans and Jewish people don't get on, do they?'

'Why not?' asks Benny.

'Because Samaritans live differently to the way Jewish people live,' answers Dave. 'And Jewish people don't like them for it.'

Jesus says, 'The man from Samaria saw the robbers' victim, too. He stopped walking. Stopped and stared.

'But only for a moment.

'Then he ran.

'Did he run to the other side of the road like the others? Did he run away just as fast as his legs would carry him?

'No. When the Samaritan saw the injured man, he felt so very sorry for him that he ran straight to him! He realised that the man was more dead than alive. He went to his donkey and rummaged through his luggage to pull out some oil and some wine. Then he poured them on the terrible wounds to clean them, and he tore some cloth into strips to use as bandages.

'And when he'd finished, what then, do you think?' Jesus asks. 'Did he ride away? Did he think, "Well, that's it. I've done all I can do"?

'Again, no! The Samaritan lifted the man up from the ground and placed him on his donkey. With the donkey carrying him, the Samaritan took him along the road until he found an inn. Then he helped him inside, and there he took care of him.

'The next day, the Samaritan did have to be on his way,' Jesus adds. 'But before he left, he gave two silver coins – out of his own money – to the innkeeper and said, "Please look after this man. If you have to spend any more on him, then keep a note of it and I'll pay you back when I come through this way again. Just help him to get better."'

There is silence.

The story is finished and all the listeners seem lost for words.

Jesus' gaze still rests on the questioner in front of Him. 'Now,' He says, 'you've heard my story. You tell me which of the three men you think behaved as a neighbour to the wounded man.'

The teacher of the Law's eyes flick towards Jesus' disciples. They watch him; wait for him to speak.

THERE IS ONLY ONE ANSWER.

'The one who takes care of him,' he replies finally.

'Yes!' smiles Jesus. 'So you go now and behave in the very same way.'

The man fidgets uncomfortably for a moment.
He wants to say more, but there is no more to say.

And he turns and strides away.

Benny nudges Dave. 'So, the Samaritan was a neighbour to the wounded man,' he says. 'But – the Samaritan must have seen the wounded man as *his* neighbour, too. I mean, he was a Jew, right?

Someone the Samaritan didn't get along with. But he was still a person. And a person who needed his help.'

Dave nods. 'The Samaritan would have been the last person in the world you'd think would have stopped to help a Jewish man. Jesus is saying that we're all neighbours to each other. We should *all* look out for each other *all* the time. **WE SHOULD BE READY TO HELP ANYONE.** It doesn't matter who they are or how their lives are different from ours.'

'Love God and love your neighbour,' smiles Josie. 'That's what God wants us to do. And if you love God, you'll *want* to love other people. It's just what I said,' she shrugs. 'God is all about love. And because He loves us so much, then when we love Him back – we can be with Him always. *Always.*'

CHAPTER 5
At His Feet
(Luke 10:38–42)

Jesus and His disciples stroll on into the village.
Topz amble along behind. The buildings nestle together,
squat and pale, gleaming in the glare of the sunshine.

'I really need water,' Benny moans. 'My mouth feels
like a desert after all that rolling.'

'A desert!' grins Danny. 'Bit of an exaggeration
there, Benny.'

Benny shakes his head firmly. 'It really does feel as
dry as a desert, actually. I never want to roll down a
hill again. It makes you thirsty *and* sick! And who even
knows when I'll get my appetite back? I may never feel
hungry again!'

Just then, Topz notice Jesus leave His disciples and
turn up an alleyway by Himself. The Gang follow after
Him. Down another street and outside a house a few
buildings along, Jesus stops. He's barely raised a hand
to knock at the door when a woman rushes out.

'Jesus!' she cries. She beams all over her face.
'Come in, come in! Mary's just inside. You'll have to
forgive the mess, I'm afraid. We've been working away,

but we're still not done. Haven't even finished getting a meal ready.'

'A meal,' Benny murmurs. 'Sounds good.'

Sarah laughs at him. 'Got your appetite back really quite quickly, then.'

The woman ushers Jesus inside the house. 'Mary!' she calls. 'Mary! He's here. Jesus! Come on, He's arrived.'

Almost at once, Mary bustles into the room. She claps her hands together in delight. Her eyes shine. She doesn't try to hide her excitement at Jesus' visit. All the chores she could be getting on with are forgotten at the sight of Him. She simply offers Him a seat and then **PLONKS HERSELF DOWN ON THE FLOOR IN FRONT OF HIM**.

Jesus starts to talk to her – to teach her. She has heard Him teach before, of course she has, but she knows how special His teaching is. How important it is to listen because every word He speaks matters. And she clings to each one; soaks them up. She barely notices that her sister, Martha, hasn't sat down with her.

She doesn't realise that Martha isn't even in the room.

All she cares about is listening to Jesus. Being close to her Lord.

Until – 'Mary!'

Martha's voice is sharp. Cross. There are tired lines on her face.

'Is that it then, Mary?' she snaps. 'You've downed tools for the day, have you?'

Mary goes to speak but Martha flaps a hand at her to be quiet.

'No, that's fine, Mary!' she grumbles on. 'You just sit down there and do nothing. Never mind that the house is still a tip, there are clothes to be washed and there's no meal on the table. I mean, what's Jesus supposed to eat? Fresh air? And you, Lord,' she continues. 'You're very welcome in this house, You know You are. But there are jobs to be done. Aren't You bothered that Mary's just sitting there doing nothing? Just sitting and leaving it all to me? Why should I have to get on with everything all by myself? It's not fair, is it? Tell her to get up and come and give me a hand!'

Mary fidgets uncomfortably. She glances at Martha; glances at Jesus awkwardly. What a show of bad temper! What must He think?

Jesus shakes His head. Not angrily. Not because He thinks Martha should be quiet while He's talking or that Mary is lazy. Instead His eyes are full of warmth and kindness and a smile twitches at the corners of His mouth.

'Martha!' he says. 'Oh, Martha! You're always so busy, aren't you? Always worried about this, always stressed about that.

'Well, let me tell you – there is only one thing that's important today. Only one thing that matters right at this moment. That is to put away your work and to sit and listen to me. *I HAVE INCREDIBLE THINGS TO TEACH YOU.* About God! And I want you both to hear them.

'Martha,' Jesus adds softly, 'Mary has chosen to spend the time I am here – in your house – with me.

It's the right thing to do. And I'm not going to tell her to do anything different.'

Outside, the afternoon sun creeps around the rooftops; sinks a little lower in the cloudless sky.

'Shall we go and get something to eat?' Paul asks.

'Thought you'd never ask,' says Benny.

Josie's eyes still rest on Mary and Martha's house.

'**IMAGINE IF JESUS KNOCKED ON YOUR DOOR** and wanted to come in and spend some time with you,' she murmurs. 'Imagine if He was just there, in your house. Just wanting to talk to you.'

Dave smiles. 'But that *is* what He wants, isn't it? Time to talk to us and for us to make time to listen to Him. That's what He's here for. To be *with* us. To teach us how to be friends with Him and with God.'

Josie continues to gaze at the house across the street. The house where Jesus is. Where right at this moment, He talks to His two friends. Where Martha and Mary are learning that the best way to spend precious time is by listening to Him.

And sitting at His feet.

CHAPTER 6

Always

(Luke 11:5–8)

John swims.

He reaches the far bank of the river for the fifth time, tumble turns and heads back to the other side. His arms swing round. His hands dig down into the water – one then the other, one then the other – dragging him along. As his legs kick they propel him forwards, frothing a trail behind him.

On the other bank, Gruff tears up and down in excitement. He barks at everything; barks at nothing. Every so often he stops dead still, one front paw raised. His ears are lifted, alert. His cold, black nose twitches as it searches the air. Then the mad running begins again.

John completes his final width. Breathless, he slams an arm down onto the grass to anchor himself to the bank. In no time, Gruff is all over him, leaping around his head, licking his face.

'Stop it, Gruff! Enough!' he squeals.

He pulls himself out of the water and rolls onto his back, still gasping for breath. Gruff ignores his command. Tail wagging wildly, he shoves his nose into

John's face and keeps licking him. John's raised arms do nothing to protect him.

'Sarah!' John yells. 'Sarah, get him off!'

Sarah shrugs her shoulders. 'How am I supposed to do that? He's your dog.'

'Yeah, but he's not listening to me, is he?' John splutters.

'And since when did Gruff *ever* listen to you? All right, hold on a minute.'

Sarah holds Saucy in her arms, who watches Gruff's antics curiously, as if she can't quite make him out. Pulling at the opening of the bag that's slung across her body, Sarah slips the little cat carefully inside. Saucy instantly wriggles her head upwards so that she can see out.

'Hurry up!' wails John. 'I'm being licked to pieces here!'

Before Sarah can grab Gruff's collar, a long, clear whistle pierces the air.

Instantly Gruff freezes.

'Go on then, boy!' a voice calls.

A short, stubby piece of stick flies upwards in a wide arc. Gruff spots it; immediately chases after it. And John grabs his chance and scrambles quickly to his feet.

He rubs the backs of his hands over his face. 'Thought he was never going to stop.'

A boy stands grinning at him on the bank.

'Thanks, Isaac,' John says.

Gruff pelts back, stick in mouth. He looks from John to Isaac, tail madly beating the air. For a moment he seems undecided. Then he drops it at Isaac's feet.

Isaac, Topz' friend from the fishing village,

Capernaum, raises his eyebrows at the eager, furry face looking up at him.

'Again?' he asks. 'All right then, again,' and he stoops, picks up the stick and hurls it along the riverbank once more.

John steps towards the dry clothes he's left in a heap on the grass. He shakes them out and starts to put them back on.

'And thanks to you, too, Sarah,' he says. 'Remind me never to rely on *you* in a crisis.'

Sarah wrinkles her nose. 'Gruff was licking you, that's hardly a crisis, John. Anyway, he's your dog. You ought to have him under control.'

'Yes, we all know what I *ought* to do,' argues John. 'But this is Gruff we're talking about. Gruff, the only dog in the whole world ever with complete un-trainability.'

Gruff is back again at Isaac's feet, the stick clasped in his jaws.

'I wouldn't say *complete* un-trainability,' Isaac says. 'Gruff – drop the stick.'

Without hesitating, Gruff lets the stick fall from his mouth. He shuffles backwards slightly, doesn't take his eyes from it. Waits. Even as Isaac bends to pick it up, he doesn't try to snatch it. He doesn't move again until Isaac has hurled it for the third time as hard as he can. It spins upwards. Then away the dog runs, eyes glued to the stick's path through the air.

'Yeah, well, that's just showing off,' John grunts.

Isaac's eyes twinkle as he laughs.

John rubs his hands through his hair to brush out the last drops of river water. 'I've been swimming widths,' he adds. 'Sarah was timing me.'

He glances at her; waits for her to tell him how fast he was.

Sarah's eyes flick from John to Isaac. 'Oh,' she says.

'Oh?' frowns John. 'You were going to count the seconds. Didn't you do it?'

'I started to,' says Sarah. 'But then I got distracted.'

'By what?' John raises his eyes. 'I was swimming my heart out just then.'

'I know and I'm sorry,' Sarah answers. 'It's just Saucy kept batting at me with her paws. It's not easy to count seconds when you're being batted by Saucy's paws. Sometimes I think I should call her Batty, not Saucy.'

'Sometimes I think I should call *you* Batty, not Sarah,' grunts John.

The three of them wander away from the riverside and find the rest of the Gang just through the trees.

They find Jesus there, too. He sits a little way ahead of them on a grassy mound. His disciple friends sit around Him.

'Imagine this,' Jesus is saying. 'It's midnight. A friend of yours has just knocked on your door. So you pop over to another friend's house and tell him, "A friend of mine is on his travels and has just arrived unexpectedly at my house. Trouble is, I've got no food to give him."

'Now,' Jesus goes on, 'supposing your friend answers from behind his closed door, "Don't you go knocking on my door at this time of night! I've already bolted it shut and my children and I have gone to bed. I'm not going to open up and give you anything now."'

Jesus pauses; glances round at His listeners.

'Well?' He asks. 'How do you think this story ends? You see, that person you've woken, he might not give you any bread just because you are a friend. But he *will* disturb himself and give you all that you need because you're not afraid to keep asking for it.'

'Is He talking about God?' Isaac whispers. 'I don't get it, God *is* our Friend. He *is* our Friend, isn't He?'

'Always,' Paul answers. 'I think Jesus means that when we go to God – when we ask Him for what we need – He doesn't just answer us because we're friends. He answers us because we keep going to Him. We keep asking.'

'God wants us to rely on Him for everything,' Sarah says. 'That means we need to go to Him all the time. We need to talk to Him every day. The more we go to God, the more serious He'll see we are about Him. About living our lives for Him.'

Paul nods his head; looks back at Jesus and the men with Him.

Jesus stands. As He walks away, His friends get to their feet, too, and follow after Him.

'We've just got to never give up, Isaac,' Paul says. 'As long as we never give up on Him, as long as we keep trusting, as long as we keep on *asking* Him for what we need – then **GOD WILL ALWAYS ANSWER**. It might not be straightaway and He might not always say yes. But He *will* always answer.'

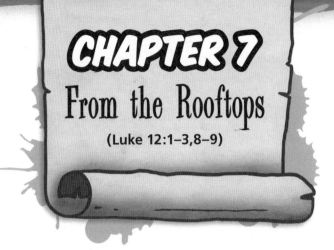

CHAPTER 7
From the Rooftops
(Luke 12:1–3,8–9)

Isaac is wide awake.

He fidgets. He lies on one side and then rolls over to lie on the other. He stretches out on his back, eyes open; eyes closed. He tries to keep his mind still; tries to calm the thoughts that tumble about, one on top of the other, inside his head. He tries to relax.

But sleep doesn't come.

Whether his eyes are wide open or tight shut, he still pictures himself in the crowd. That dense huddle of people from earlier in the day. Pushing and jostling and straining to hear, straining to see. Desperate to catch the words Jesus speaks to His disciples.

And as people press in around Isaac, shove him, as he feels hot and stifled and hardly able to breathe in the crush – he hears each one.

Suddenly, he sits upright on his bed.

No point lying there anymore. No point trying to sleep. His head pounds. His heart seems to race too quickly. Not a square inch of his mattress feels comfortable or invites him to stay tucked up where he is.

Quietly, he gets up. He pulls his blanket around him and creeps out of the room. His parents are asleep. Isaac can hear their breathing. Steady and deep and slow. He creeps on tiptoe so as not to wake them. He steals outside into the street.

The night is silent. Still.

No candles burn in house windows. No voices carry on the fresh, cool air.

Isaac looks towards the moon. It washes the village in a soft, clear glow of silver.

'Just the moon and me,' he thinks. 'And the rest of Capernaum fast asleep.'

Isaac gathers the blanket around him. He fixes his eyes on the moon's face, round and full above his head.

He whispers to God.

I'm here, God. I'm here with You and the moon. And I need You to be here with me. I need to talk to You. Jesus says that if we keep asking, You will answer. If we go on asking for what we need, You will give it to us.

Well, what I need tonight is You, God. What I need is for You to listen to me.

I heard Jesus talking again today. I was in a huge crowd. There were so many people pushing and shoving, trying to get close enough to listen. And I didn't like it. I didn't like being shoved into. I didn't like it that the crowd was so thick this time that I couldn't get out of it.

But at the same time, I didn't want to get out. I wanted to stay where I was. I wanted to be close to Jesus. I didn't want to miss what He had to say.

Jesus spoke about the Pharisees, God. He said that we should be careful of them. Careful not to listen to what they say. He said that they are hypocrites. They teach as if they know all about You but they don't speak about Your love or Your forgiveness. Not the way Jesus does. They talk only about the rules we should live by. And they don't believe that You sent Jesus to us. They don't accept the things He says.

And Jesus said they say things they shouldn't say and they do things they shouldn't do – when they think no one is listening and no one is watching. But they forget, don't they, God? They forget that You are everywhere! You are all around and You see everything. You hear everything.

Jesus said there is nothing that can be hidden from You. Not one word. Not one secret. Nothing can be covered up because You will uncover it. And anything muttered when it's dark and there's no one around will be heard in the bright light of the daytime when there are people everywhere. Anything whispered behind a closed door will be shouted out loud from the rooftops!

But then Jesus said there are things that MUST be shouted from the rooftops, too. Things we mustn't keep quiet about. He said that if we tell people that we belong to Him – tell people that we are Your friends and that we love You – then He will do the same for us. He will tell Your angels that we are His and so we'll be safe with You forever.

Isaac stops talking. He shivers. He pulls the blanket more tightly around him. A frown wrinkles his forehead as a thin cloud drifts across the face of the moon.

Jesus said something else, though. He said that if we do the opposite – if we tell people that we're not Your friends and we don't want to have anything to do with You – then He'll tell Your angels that we're nothing to do with Him either.

And wouldn't that be so terrible? Because then You wouldn't be with us and we wouldn't be with You. Not here on earth and not in heaven.

So what I want to say, God, is that I never want to be without You. Not ever. Not for a single second of a single day. Will You help me?

Please help me remember that You are everywhere. That You hear every word I say, even when I'm not actually speaking to You. That You see everything I do, even when it's something ordinary. Something just simple, like sweeping the floor or feeding my donkey. Nothing is hidden from You.

Let the things I say and the things I do be things that make You happy, God.

And please, if anyone asks me about You – or if I meet anyone who needs to know You – please help me to be brave enough to tell them, 'Yes, Jesus is the Son of God! Yes, God is my Friend – and **HE CAN BE YOUR FRIEND, TOO!***'*

Let me never be afraid to shout Your name from the rooftops. And let me never be ashamed to hear You shout the things I do and the things I say from the rooftops either.

I want to be with You, God!

Help me to listen to You.

Teach me to obey You.

Hold on to me.

Forever.

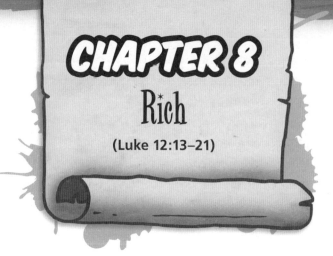

CHAPTER 8
Rich
(Luke 12:13–21)

'There! Over there!'

Danny points. Over the heads of the crowd, he can see Dave jumping up and down and waving his arms.

Paul screws up his eyes. 'What?' Even through his glasses, he still can't make out the bouncing, waving Topz boy.

'It's Dave, come on,' says Danny.

'Where?' Paul asks, still peering. 'How can you see Dave? And come to think of it,' he adds, trying to keep up with Danny's determined shove through the crowd, 'how can Dave see *us*? There must be hundreds of people here. This is a people forest, Danny. An actual forest of people.'

'Topz radar!' Danny calls back to him. 'Never lets us down!'

Jesus is teaching and Dave has managed to grab a perfect spot; close enough to Him to be able to hear easily, and just high enough up on a rise in the ground to get a good view of Him over people's heads. There's barely space, but Danny and Paul squash up close to each other and somehow cram themselves onto the grassy mound next to him.

A little way away from them, a well-dressed man tries to get close to Jesus, too. It's a struggle. It takes him quite some time to weave himself through the onlookers to the front of the crowd. People stare at him as he shoves past. They mutter, 'Who does he think he is, pushing in like that?' At last, he gets close enough to the front to be able to make himself heard.

'Teacher!' the man calls. His voice is sharp. He doesn't look happy. If anything, he looks in a bad temper.

'Teacher, my father has left some property to us – to me and to my brother. Tell my brother to split it with me.'

Jesus gazes at the man a moment. His eyes twinkle. He seems almost amused.

'I'm not sure who you take me for, my friend,' He says. 'Do you think someone has given me the right to divide up property – to decide who should get what?'

Without waiting for the man to answer, Jesus looks out towards the crowd. He scans the faces, the eager eyes all fixed on Him.

'However rich you are,' He says, 'it's not the things you own that matter. Who you are isn't all about wealth. It isn't all about what you *have*. That's not what God wants for you. That's not what He wants to find deep inside you. You must watch out! You must take care that having lots of "things" doesn't become more important to you than anything else. You must make sure you don't get greedy!'

'Am I greedy, Dave?' Danny hisses. 'I don't think I am. I don't mean to be. I do like having "things", though.'

'No.' Dave shakes his head. 'Jesus doesn't mean it's greedy to have stuff. He means you can have stuff *without* being greedy.'

'Yeah,' adds Paul. 'If all you care about is having lots of things and how to get *more* things, then that's being greedy. But if you try to remember that God has given you everything you have, then you'll be more likely to share it. You'll want to use what you have the way God asks you to.'

'I have a story for you,' Jesus announces. Again, He doesn't just talk to the man in front of Him. He talks to the crowd. 'Once, there was a rich man. He owned plenty of land. The soil was good and the crops he planted always did very well.

'So well, in fact,' Jesus continues, 'that after a while he had grown so much food, he didn't know what to do with it all.

'"Well, fancy that!" the man thinks to himself. "My crops are magnificent, but I haven't enough space to keep all this food. What am I going to do?"

'Then, "I know!" he cries. "I shall pull down the barns I have that are too small, and build new barns that are much bigger! I'll make sure they are plenty large enough to store all my corn and the rest of my harvest, too. And *then*," the man smiled, "I shall have everything I need to live comfortably for a very long time. I shall be able to sit back and relax. Plenty to eat. Plenty to drink. What fun!"'

'Huh!' murmurs Paul. 'Well, that *is* greedy!'

'That can't be the end of it,' Danny whispers. 'If that man's got way more than he needs, God will want him to share it. What about poor people who have hardly any food at all? He should give them some of it rather than keeping it all for himself.'

It's as if Jesus has heard him. For one moment – the tiniest moment – Danny's sure that Jesus' gaze turns to rest on him; that a half smile lifts a corner of His mouth. Then His eyes flick back to the crowd.

'Do you think God is happy with this?' He asks. 'No! He's not happy at all! He says to the man, "What a fool you are! Well, think about this, will you? You've come to the end of your life. This night will be your very last! So what will happen to all the things you've stored up for yourself? Who's going to enjoy them now?"'

Jesus pauses. He gives His listeners a moment to think about His story. He lets His words sink in.

'You can pile up as many riches – as many "things" – as you want to,' He says. 'But that doesn't make you rich in God's eyes. God wants you to put Him first. To put other people's needs before your own. And let me tell you,' He adds, 'being rich like that in God's eyes is the only sort of richness that matters.'

Dave watches the well-dressed man who has pushed his way to the front of the crowd. He still looks cross; still seems to wait to have his family quarrel sorted out for him.

'If we're rich in God's eyes,' Dave says, 'we're richer than anything, because we have God as a Friend.

IT'S ALL ABOUT MAKING HIM THE CENTRE OF EVERYTHING. Every day.'

'Which is hard,' says Danny, 'because sometimes I don't feel like it. Do you? Sometimes I want to do things my way, not God's way. I want everything to be all about me and not all about Him.'

'Yeah, but if we don't give up trying,' says Paul, 'if we *can* put Him first, then we *will* live the way God asks us to. We'll *want* to. Because we love Him.'

CHAPTER 9
Ready?
(Luke 12:35–40)

'Room for two more?'

Dave turns his head. Josie and Sarah stand just below the grassy mound where he's wedged between Paul and Danny. The girls have managed to work their way around the edge of the crowd, but they can't see Jesus.

Dave glances right and left. 'Not really,' he says. 'Not sure we can all scrunch up any tighter.'

'Oh, you can!' says Josie. 'There's only two of us.'

'Well, three,' adds Sarah. 'If you include Saucy.'

A woman swivels as far as she can in the thick huddle to look at her.

'Saucy? Now there's a name!' she laughs. 'And where is she, this Saucy?'

'Erm … she's here,' Sarah smiles.

She lifts the bag that hangs over her shoulder. The woman peers into it; claps her hands together.

'Oh! It's a cat!' she cries. 'Would you look at that? Then it's a perfect name!'

Sarah chuckles. 'Listen,' says the woman, 'why don't you pop up here in my space?'

Josie shakes her head. 'Oh, no, we couldn't do that.'

'Of course you could,' beams the woman. 'I'm offering, aren't I? I should be on my way. I've bread to bake and a pile of clothes to mend. My husband's. He's a fisherman. He's always getting them caught on that boat of his. Besides, if I move, there'll be plenty of room for the two of you – I mean the three of you. I must be twice the size round the middle as the pair of you two girls put together!'

The woman eases herself down from the little mound. At the same time, the Topz girls step up and squeeze into the space she leaves next to Danny, Paul and Dave.

They turn to thank her. She's already bustling away, one handed lifted in a wave.

'You listen to that Man, Jesus,' she calls back to them. 'If ever a man was worth listening to, it's Him!'

The numbers of onlookers continue to grow. People join on all sides. The sea of bodies and eager faces stretches further and further back; spreads wider and wider.

'What have we missed?' the newcomers want to know. They can't see Jesus. They can't hear Him either. Not properly, they're too far away. They have to make do with having His words retold to them as His stories are passed back through the crowd by those who are closer to Him.

'Are you ready?' Jesus calls out. 'You must be ready for whatever happens! You must make sure you are dressed for action. You must see to it that your lamps are lit so that you're not caught out in the dark.'

He pauses a moment; gathers His thoughts.

'Do you know what you must be like?' He continues. 'You must be like servants – good, hardworking and faithful servants. Servants who wait patiently for their master to come back home after a wedding party.

'Imagine it!' cries Jesus. 'He comes back to his house, knocks on the door, and straightaway those servants run to let him in.

'And good for them that they do! Good for them that their master finds them wide awake and ready to serve him, even though it's late!

'Because that master will reward his faithful servants,' Jesus says. 'He will take his coat off, he will ask them to sit down, and then *he* will serve *them*. You see? How good for those servants it will be if he gets home at midnight, or later, to find them still up, still ready and waiting for him.

'And what about the owner of a house?' He goes on. 'If he knew he was going to be burgled, if he knew exactly what time the thief was going to break in, you can be certain that he'd do everything he could to stop that thief getting into his house.'

Jesus' eyes sweep the huge crowd in front of Him, to the sides of Him.

'Do you understand?' He asks. 'I want you to understand. It's all about being ready! Ready for the Son of Man to come back, because He will! And He will come back when you least expect Him.'

'But He's here,' murmurs Josie. She gazes at Him as He stands there, right in front of her eyes. 'The Son of Man is here. Now. It's Jesus.'

Paul shakes his head. 'I know. Weird. He can't come back if He hasn't gone anywhere.'

'I remember something.' Sarah's voice sounds small. Far away somehow. As if it's coming from deep inside her.

'What do you remember?' asks Josie.

'Something John told me. Something he heard Jesus say. Something awful but … something incredible.'

In the bag, Saucy rubs her head against Sarah's ribs. Absently, Sarah lifts a hand to fondle her cat's ears. But her eyes are distant. They barely see what's around her. They seem instead to focus on something a long way off.

'If we're going to be ready,' she says slowly, 'we have to live our lives the way God wants us to. Not just every now and then, but every day. Always. We have to do as He asks us to. We have to obey Him.

'We have to be ready to serve Him, too. Just like the servants waiting for their master to come home, we have to be ready to serve God. Any time and in any place. And like Jesus says, we don't know if a burglar's going to break into our houses, but we need to be ready in case someone tries. We have to live God's way all the time, not just when we feel like it.'

'I get that,' Danny replies. 'But it's the being ready part. If we've got to make sure we're ready – then ready for what?'

'Jesus told us – ready for Him to come back.'

Josie laughs. 'But He's here, Sarah. Right here. Look!'

Sarah's mouth feels dry. She doesn't want it to be true. This thing she knows. This thing John overheard. She wishes he'd never told her.

But he has.

'Sarah, where's He coming back from?'

'Death,' Sarah whispers. 'The people who don't like what Jesus says – the Pharisees and the chief priests and all of them, the ones who hate Him –'

The words catch in her throat.

'THEY'RE GOING TO KILL HIM.'

CHAPTER 10
When Rules Don't Apply
(Luke 13:10–17)

Benny has a headache.

It was there when he woke up in the morning. A dull throbbing in his temples.

'You should drink plenty of water,' says Sarah. 'That always helps me when I have a headache.'

'But you know what would *really* help?' grins Dave. 'Leapfrog race. Down by the lake.'

Benny narrows his eyes, gives his friend a sideways glance.

'Dave,' he mutters, 'do you have any idea what a headache actually is?'

'Yeah,' nods Dave. 'A pain in the head.'

Benny scowls. 'So exactly how is leapfrogging around at the lake going to help?'

'Dunno,' Dave shrugs. 'But it'll give you something else to think about.'

'No, it won't,' Benny grunts.

'Oh ... Well, do you mind if we go and leapfrog anyway? You could sit and watch.'

'No.' Benny shakes his head, then immediately wishes he hadn't. 'I'll just go for a little walk. Find somewhere shady to sit. It'll be too hot on the beach.'

'Do you want me to stay with you?' asks Josie.

'No,' Benny says again. 'But thanks.'

Sarah scrambles to her feet and follows the other Topz as they wander out of the village, towards the lake.

'Water, Benny,' she calls over her shoulder. 'Drink lots of water.'

Putting his hands to his head, Benny closes his eyes and gently massages his aching temples.

'I've got some water if you want some.'

His eyes flick open again. He squints upwards.

Isaac stands between him and the sun.

'Thanks.' Benny smiles. He reaches for the leather pouch that Isaac holds out, tilts it to his mouth and swallows some water.

Isaac crouches beside him.

'You look rough,' he says.

'Nah,' Benny replies. He hands the pouch back. 'Just a headache. Thanks for the drink.'

There's a stillness in the village. A hush instead of the usual hustle and bustle.

It's the Sabbath day.

God's day.

'Do you feel like a wander?' Benny asks.

'Yes,' Isaac nods. 'I was just wandering anyway.'

The two boys stand up. Benny gives himself a stretch, rolls his head gently from side to side. Then they begin to amble along the street. Through the empty marketplace.

They pass small children playing, people talking with friends and neighbours. All very calm.

There's a sense of quiet in the air. Something relaxed and unhurried. Peaceful.

Benny and Isaac walk along shady alleys, and the shadows and the day of rest soothe Benny's aching head.

The synagogue doors stand open. There are people milling at the entrance. They can't get inside. The building is already packed.

It's packed because Jesus is there. Teaching.

'We could stand there, too,' suggests Isaac. 'Try to hear what's going on. Do you want to? It's cool near the doorway. Out of the sun.'

Benny smiles at him. 'Sounds good.'

They cross the street. As they join the people who cluster about the doorway, suddenly something like a cheer explodes from within the synagogue building. Those inside begin to praise God at the tops of their voices!

The sound is astonishing.

What Jesus has done must be even more astonishing still!

'What is it?'

'What's happened?'

'I wish we could see in there!'

'Can anyone tell us what's going on?'

'Come on, what have we missed?'

The murmurs and mutters run all through the crowd at the synagogue door.

'Please, someone! Someone tell us! What's happened?'

The story of the miracle begins to spread back and back through the onlookers; words pass from one to the other, as those who can see and hear explain excitedly what Jesus has done. What Jesus has said.

At last the news bursts outside. As if the walls of the building simply can't contain it anymore.

A man close to the open doorway turns. His eyes sparkle. His face shines.

'There's a woman in there!' he cries. He sounds breathless. Full of wonder. 'She was sick. She was so ill that for eighteen years – *eighteen years!* – she was all bent over. She just couldn't straighten up. Not at all.

'Jesus was teaching and she was right down the front. He saw her. He looked right at her. He called to her. Called out to her in front of everyone.

'"Woman!" He said. "You'll be all right now. You're free from this sickness." And then He placed His hands on her.

'And at once – at absolute once – she was better. She was cured! She stood up as straight as you and me! And how the praises to God just poured out of her mouth!'

The man pauses a moment, as if he needs time to grasp what he's saying.

'Well, don't stop there!' smiles a woman next to him. 'What about the official?'

She glances behind her. Where's the man she's talking about? Should she tell? Is it alright to say?

Turning back, she hisses, 'The official in there, he was angry with Jesus! He was cross with Him because He'd made someone better on the Sabbath day. So he said to all the people who'd seen what Jesus had done, "We have six days when we can do our work. If you want to be healed, come to the synagogue on one of those days. But don't come on the Sabbath!"

'But Jesus, He wasn't going to keep quiet, was He? He told that official, and the others in there with him, that he was a hypocrite! Said it in front of everybody, He did!

'Jesus said, "There's not one of you who wouldn't take your ox or your donkey from its stable on the Sabbath, so you could lead it outside for a drink of water. Not one of you! Yet here is a woman who has suffered with such sickness for eighteen years of her life that she couldn't even stand up straight. So why shouldn't she be set free today? **WHY SHOULDN'T SHE BE MADE WELL AGAIN ON THE SABBATH DAY?**"

'And then, didn't the crowd cheer!' the woman beams. 'Well, you all heard them, didn't you? You couldn't have *not* heard them! Cheering and praising God fit to raise the roof, they were!

'But those officials – well! They looked like they wanted the floor to swallow them up, they were so ashamed.'

The people at the synagogue door laugh and cheer, as if they are seeing the miracle for themselves. As if Jesus has healed the woman in front of their own eyes.

'Where is she then?' someone asks. 'Where's the woman who's all better? I want to see her. I want to meet her. I want to know how it feels to have the power of God rushing through you like that!'

Isaac nudges Benny. 'Sabbath day rules don't apply to God's love, do they?' he smiles. 'God wants people to have a rest from doing their work but not from caring about each other. He means us to care about each other and help each other, if we can, every day of the week. Doesn't He?'

'Yup,' nods Benny. 'Jesus never turns His back on someone who needs Him. No matter when that is or where it is. And God never stops giving Jesus the power He needs to do good things – whether it's the Sabbath day or not.'

'How's your headache?' asks Isaac.

'It's, erm ... it's better.' Benny raises his eyebrows in surprise and grins. 'We must have cheered it away.'

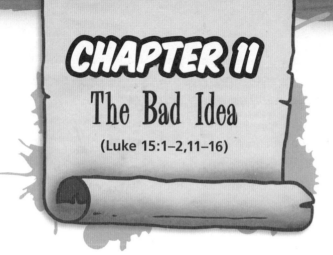

CHAPTER 11
The Bad Idea
(Luke 15:1–2,11–16)

Josie scowls. She can't help it.

Dave gives her hair a playful tug.

'What's up with you?' he asks. 'You look like even your bad mood's in a bad mood.'

'Listen to them!' Josie hisses. 'Just listen!'

Dave glances around. Josie stands on the very edge of a mass of people all gathered to hear Jesus talk.

All sorts of people.

Rich and poor. Those with important jobs and those with the lowest paid jobs going. The ones who think very highly of themselves and the ones who are hated and ignored – like the tax collectors, who most people wouldn't be seen dead even talking to.

'There's a lot of people here, Josie,' Dave says. 'Give me a clue. Which ones am I supposed to be listening to?'

'Those!' Josie spits out the word. 'The grumblers!'

She jerks her head, fixing her eyes on a cluster of men who stand a little apart from the rest of the crowd.

Dave knows who they are. Most people know who they are. They are men who like to be recognised; who want to be looked up to.

These are Pharisees and teachers of the Law.

Men who don't like Jesus one bit.

'They never stop!' Josie frowns. 'Always complaining. Jesus has come to teach everyone because God wants *everyone* to know how much He loves them and wants to be their Friend. It doesn't matter who you are – how poor or how ordinary or ... how *bad*! That's not how God looks at people. And Jesus has said that over and over again, only they're not listening. They're doing it again right now. Moaning because Jesus is friends with the people no one else wants to know.'

Josie throws back her shoulders. She tosses her head, deepens her voice to mimic the Pharisees: 'Who does this Man think He is? He spends time with such dreadful people. He even goes and has dinner with them ...'

'Sssh!' Dave puts a finger to his lips. 'Do you really want them to hear you?'

'Don't think I care if they do,' Josie shrugs. 'I don't know how Jesus puts up with them.'

Dave smiles. 'Probably because He's *Jesus*. He'll never give up. He'll keep trying to explain it to them. Even if they never get it. Even if He *knows* they'll never get it. Because He loves them, Josie.'

People begin to shush one another. Jesus stands up at the front of the crowd, arms spread wide.

'I have a story to tell you,' He says. 'All of you – are you listening?'

Josie glances again at the grumblers. 'If only *they'd* listen,' she murmurs.

'This story,' Jesus begins, 'is about a man and his two sons. Now the younger son said to his father, "One day, everything you own – the house, the farm, all of it – will be handed down to me and to my brother. Well, Father," said the young lad, "I don't want to wait! I want my share of what will come to me, right now."

'However the boy's father felt about this, he did as his son had asked. He spent time working out what was what, did the whole thing properly – and gave his son his fair share of everything he owned.

'What did his father think his son would do with it? Who knows? But what the boy *did* do, just a few days later, was sell all that he'd been given. Every last bit. Then, with a sack full of money, he packed up and he left home. He even left the country and went somewhere a long, long way away.

'You see, this boy dreamed of a new life. A life away from his father's farm. A life where he wouldn't have to work. Where he could just spend his time – and his money – enjoying himself. So that's what he did.

'He enjoyed lots of food; he enjoyed lots to drink. He threw party after party. He splashed his money about as if he had an endless supply. And he thought he was pretty happy.'

Dave shakes his head. 'Something tells me this isn't going to end well, Josie.'

'Of course, when you spend money like that,' says Jesus, 'when you're so careless with it – well – the time's bound to come when it runs out. And the time came when it ran out for the young lad. Every last coin, until the sack was completely empty.'

'Told you,' whispers Dave.

'And his money isn't the only thing to run out,' Jesus continues. 'So does most of the food in the country where he's chosen to live. A famine hits and it's bad. And the boy ends up with nothing at all.

'So, he does the only thing he can. He goes out to look for work, and finds himself working once more on a farm. The very thing he thought he'd escaped from! Only it's not his father's farm. And this time it's his job to look after the pigs.

'He's miserable but he does it. He has no choice. He trudges about in the mud; he breathes in the stinking air. And he's so hungry he even wishes he could eat the revolting looking food that the pigs gobble up.'

Jesus stops His storytelling a moment.

The sun has climbed high in the sky. Only a few twists and rags of cloud hang in the wash of blue overhead. There's no breath of wind and they scarcely move. The heat beats down on the onlookers – on the eager listeners and the sour-faced grumblers.

What will *they* make of the end of this story? The ones who hate Him; the ones who want Him to disappear, who wish He'd never turned up in the first place. Will they ever understand?

Josie is sad for them if they don't.

Sad for anyone who doesn't turn away from the wrong things they do and start again with God.

Because **GOD SITS, WAITING TO WELCOME EVERYONE**.

With an open heart and with open arms.

'So?' Jesus asks. 'What do you think? Whatever will become of that foolish young boy? What is he going to do now?'

CHAPTER 12
The Happy Ending
(Luke 15:17–32)

The people wait.

They wait for Jesus to speak again.

'The boy in my story had no money,' Jesus says. 'He'd spent the lot. Everything that his father had agreed to give him. He'd wasted it all away. Even the pigs had more to eat than he did.

'But that's when he realised. That's when he saw – finally! – how stupid he'd been.

'"You idiot!" he muttered to himself. "The people who work for my father – they never go hungry. He makes sure of it. He takes care of them.

'"And look at me! I'm on the point of starving to death!

'"So here's what I'm going to do. I'm going to get out of here. I'm going to leave this country far behind and go back to my father. I'll tell him how wrong I've been. I'll say that I know I've done a terrible thing, to him and to God, by being so selfish. I'll tell him that I don't deserve to be called his son anymore. And I'll ask him just to treat me like one of his employees. To be kind enough just to give me a job. That's what I'm going to do," he said. "I'm going to go home."

'With that,' Jesus says, 'that young lad picked himself up and began the long journey back to his father.

'Now, it was quite a time since he left,' He adds. 'For all he knew, his father might have given up on him by now. He might have stopped hoping that his son would come back. He might not even care anymore.

'He *might* not ... but he did.

'Even when his son was still a long, long way away, his father spotted him – because he'd never given up looking out for him. Day after day after day. He saw how poor the boy looked. How thin and filthy and bedraggled. But, he wasn't angry with him, oh no. His heart filled up with pity for him.

'And that father ran! He ran as he hadn't run in months. In years! He ran until he gasped for breath, until he reached his lost son, and he wrapped him up in the biggest, strongest hug you can imagine! And he kissed him.

'Well, of course, the boy had his speech all rehearsed: "I've done a terrible thing, Father. Against you and against God. I don't deserve to be called your son anymore ..."

'But his father wasn't listening.

'Instead, his father called to his servants: "My son! My son is home! Bring the very best robe out here and dress him in it. Bring a ring to put on his finger and some shoes for him to wear. And then," his father continued, "start preparing food. We are going to have a feast to celebrate! For this boy – my very own son – was dead, but now he's alive again! He was completely lost, but here he is once more!"

'Well,' says Jesus, 'of course the servants obeyed at once, and the celebrations began.

'But, if you remember, there are two sons in this story. What's happened to the older one? The one who spent all the time his brother's been away being obedient to his father. Who had kept on working hard for him and did his absolute best for him. Where was he now?

'He was on his way home,' Jesus goes on. 'On his way home from a hard day's work.

'As he got close to the house, he heard the music. As he got closer still, he saw the dancing. So he called one of the servants to him.

'"What's happening?" he asked.

'"It's your brother," the servant answered. "He's come home. And all this partying, well, that's your father's idea. He's celebrating because your brother's back safely."

'At first, the older brother couldn't quite believe his ears. After everything his little brother had done, why was his father throwing a party for him? Why wasn't he furious with his foolish actions? Why wasn't he punishing him? The older brother was so cross about it that he didn't set foot inside the house. His father had to come out to *him*.

'"Please come inside. Please," his father begged.

'"Why should I?" the older son snapped. "I've worked for you all this time. I've worked for you like a slave! And have I ever disobeyed a single order? No, I haven't, and what have you ever given me? Nothing like this, Father. Nothing like a feast for me and my friends! But this *other* son of yours," he added, "the one who took what belongs to you and wasted it all – for him you throw the biggest party I've ever seen!"

'The older boy's father gazed at him a moment. "Oh, my son," he said. "You are with me every day and my heart just bursts with love for you. Everything that I have is yours.

'"But please try to understand what has happened today. **YOUR LITTLE BROTHER WAS AS GOOD AS DEAD, AND NOW HE'S ALIVE AGAIN.** He was lost, but he's been found. How could I not celebrate having him home – safe and sound?"'

Josie sucks in a deep breath and plonks herself down on the ground.

'What's wrong?' asks Dave. 'That was a good story.'

Josie nods. 'It was. It was a great story.'

'Then what is it? Why have you got the bad mood face on again?'

'Because,' Josie shrugs, 'I feel like the older brother.'

'Feel like him how?'

'He was angry because his father had forgiven his little brother,' Josie says. 'In fact, he'd not just forgiven him; he'd thrown a huge party for him.

'And the father in the story is like God, isn't he? No matter what we've done or how we've let Him down, God always forgives us. He waits for us to turn back to Him and He welcomes us home.'

'Which is amazing!' Dave says.

'Yes, it is,' agrees Josie. 'But it makes me cross that God wants to welcome *those* people home, too.'

Her eyes drift towards the group of Pharisees, the huddle of teachers of the Law. They still stand together at a distance. They've listened to Jesus' story but there are still sneers on their faces. Their mouths are still twisted with dislike and distrust.

'We just have to try to do what God does,' Dave replies. 'We all do things wrong. And God hates those things. But when we say we're sorry, He sees past them. He sees through them. He sees *us*. He sees what He loves.

'God hates it that Jesus has enemies, Josie. He hates what they say about Him and how they look at Him. But if one of those men – just *one* – was to say, "Look, God, I think I've got this all wrong. I'm sorry and I really want to be Your friend", then the partying in heaven would be so loud it'd be heard from one end of the universe to the other!'

Dave watches as men and women and children cluster round Jesus, full of questions, full of awe and full of wonder.

'It'll always be difficult,' he says. 'Almost impossible sometimes. But we need to try to see people the way God does, Josie. *All* people, no matter what.'

Josie still gazes at the sneering men. 'I know. And God wants us to pray for them, too, doesn't He? Pray that they'll find Him. That they'll come home to Him. Even them. Even Jesus' enemies ...'

'the angels of God rejoice over one sinner who repents' (Luke 15:10)

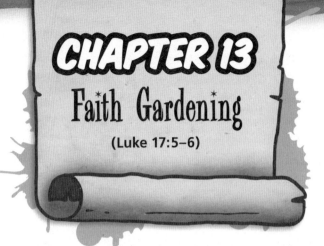

CHAPTER 13
Faith Gardening
(Luke 17:5–6)

Sarah finishes washing her face in the river for the fourth time. She inspects her clothes to make sure they're not dirty – not noticeably dirty anyway. Then she begins to work her fingers through her hair, pulling at knots, trying to smooth out the curls.

Saucy sits on a tree stump on the riverbank, watching.

'What you've got to understand, Saucy,' says Sarah, 'is that we're going to the city! This is a very big moment! We've been following Jesus, here to there and there to here – from towns to villages and back again. But now He's going to the CITY! To Jerusalem! And I've just *got* to look my best!'

Saucy blinks at her. Just once. Then she collapses down into a fluffy ball, nose tucked into her fur, and drifts off to sleep.

'Typical,' Sarah grunts.

She stops fiddling with her hair and puts her hands on her hips.

'Thanks for your support, Saucy. I mean, it's all right for you, isn't it? You spend half of every day preening, so you *always* look your best.'

'Now that explains it,' says John. 'I've always wondered how Saucy manages to look so much better than you do.'

Sarah throws him a look. 'Who asked you anyway? And for your information, I'd rather look at Gruff than at you, any day of the week.'

John grins down at his dog. 'You hear that, Gruff? Sarah thinks you're better looking than me.'

'Too right,' Sarah adds.

'Oh well,' John shrugs. 'Good job I'm *massively* intelligent with a fantastic personality, then.'

Danny steps out from among the trees with Paul at his heels.

'Are you ready to go yet, Sarah?'

'Yeah, 'cos we should really hurry,' says Paul. 'Jesus must have left by now. We need to catch up with Him.'

'So? We can catch up with Him in Jerusalem later,' says Sarah.

'Later?' Danny looks mystified. 'Erm … it's quite a long way to Jerusalem from here. We're not going to get there later today. Or tomorrow. That's why we need to follow Jesus. If we don't go after Him, we won't know which way He's gone. We won't have a clue when He's going to get there.'

'Anyway, you know what Jesus is like,' says Paul. 'He's always stopping off in different places. We could miss loads of good stuff if we lose Him now.'

Sarah looks from one Topz to the other. 'But I'm getting ready to go to Jerusalem. To the city. You said we were going to the city!'

'And we are,' Danny replies. 'Just not straightaway.'

Sarah sighs. Her eyes dart towards John. 'Did you know about this?'

'No!' He shakes his head. 'Not really … I mean … well … maybe a bit.'

'Then why didn't you say something? Why did you let me think we were going to Jerusalem today?'

'Erm …' John fidgets. 'I just thought you could do with a bit of a scrub up. That's all.'

Sarah's jaw drops but Paul doesn't give her the chance to retaliate. 'Let's just go!' He turns to head back through the trees, where the rest of the Gang wait for them. At last they can set off.

'Which way?' asks Paul.

Dave points down the road. 'It's all right, Jesus hasn't been gone long. I reckon we'll be able to see Him once we get over the hill.'

'You missed Him say the most amazing thing, though,' says Josie.

Paul stops. 'What? What did He say?'

'He said it to the disciples. They asked Him about faith. They wanted their faith to be bigger. And Jesus said, "You only need faith as big as a mustard seed. If you had just that much, you'd be able to tell that mulberry tree right there to pull itself out of the ground by the roots and go and plant itself again in the sea!"'

'A mustard seed?' says Sarah. 'That's tiny. It's almost like a bit of dust.'

'Exactly!' cries Josie. 'That's why it's so amazing! People's faith – their trust in God – it must come in all shapes and sizes. But even if you only have faith as tiny as a mustard seed, God can still do incredible things. Jesus says He can still work miracles.'

Gruff scampers on ahead of them. His small paws kick up the dust. He stops to sniff, stops to scratch. Then away he goes again, leaving a trail of little paw prints in the dirt.

'I wonder how you know how much faith you have?' John says.

Dave shrugs. 'However much you have to start with, you can always try to grow it.'

John looks at him.

'You know,' says Dave, 'like a seed. If you plant a seed and water it, and feed it with some sort of plant food or other, like my dad does, then it'll grow. It'll sprout roots and grow into a plant. And if you spend time with God – if you talk to Him and get used to trusting Him with things you're worried about – then that's a bit like watering and feeding a seed. The more times you trust God to be with you and the more you believe in Jesus' teaching about Him – well – **THE MORE YOUR FAITH WILL GROW**.'

'Oh,' nods John. 'Cool.'

Dave is first to reach the brow of the hill.

'What did I tell you? There!' He points.

Jesus strides along purposefully. His eyes look towards the horizon. Somewhere in the far distance lies Jerusalem, and He knows it's time for Him to begin His journey there. Every footstep takes Him nearer. And just like Gruff's paws, His sandals leave a trail of marks in the dust.

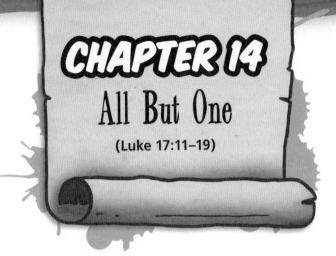

CHAPTER 14
All But One
(Luke 17:11–19)

'Where are we?' asks Paul.

'More to the point, *when* are we?' mumbles Benny. 'Feels like we've been walking for hours. I'm starving. Isn't it food time yet?'

Danny shakes his head. 'We'll stop when Jesus does. If we lose sight of Him now, we'll get lost. We'll never find Him *or* Jerusalem.'

'Which is a bit of a worry,' says Paul. 'Don't we have *any* idea where we are?'

Dave stops walking a moment. He looks around him. 'Well, I'm pretty sure,' he says, 'that over there is Galilee and on the other side of us is Samaria.'

'How sure is pretty sure?' asks Paul.

'Not very but it's all we've got.'

Paul follows Dave's gaze. 'So we're bang in the middle of the two?'

'Kind of,' nods Dave. 'Maybe. Making our way along the border, I reckon.'

Sarah is a little ahead. She pauses; peers hard into the distance. 'Is that what I think it is?'

The view isn't clear. A heat haze shimmers on the air. But the more Topz stare, the more they can make out the village. The cluster of houses, pale walls almost lost against the dusty ground.

'Stonking!' cries Benny. 'When we get there, we can stop. I mean, Jesus is bound to stop. He's got to have a rest some time.'

'And we can find out where we are,' adds Paul. 'How much further it is to Jerusalem.'

'I don't think I care,' answers Benny. 'All I want is a place to grab something to eat.'

Benny starts to run towards the village. Not fast, but a steady jog.

'It's too hot to run,' calls Josie.

He doesn't slow down. 'See you there, then!'

But almost at once, he sees what Jesus sees.

And just like Jesus, he stops completely still.

'What is it?' Josie shouts.

Benny raises an arm behind him and waves it.

'What?' Josie calls again.

'Stop!' Benny hisses.

'What? Why?'

'Just stay right there!'

A group of men have appeared. Ten of them. Benny counts them quickly. Yes. There are definitely ten.

They stand a little way away from Jesus. They look small and fragile.

They shout out to Him: 'Jesus! Oh, Jesus, Master, please have pity on us!'

Jesus stands, tall and straight and calm, and gazes at them.

Benny has seen a man like these before. All of Topz have. He knows you have to keep away from them. Far, far away. They have a terrible skin disease – that's so terribly easy to catch.

The men don't need to ask for Jesus' pity. His heart fills with sadness for them the moment He sets eyes on them.

He feels their loneliness. They can no longer live in their village; no longer be close to their family and friends. It's not allowed for fear that the infection will be passed on.

And He understands their suffering.

Jesus doesn't make a move towards them, but He calls out, 'Go and look for some priests! Ask them to have a good look at you. Go on!'

The ten men don't move either. Not for a moment. They hardly seem to understand what He's telling them to do. Is Jesus helping them or not? They stand and stare, then slowly, uncertainly, turn away.

But where will they find a priest without walking straight into the village?

The rest of the Gang step forward cautiously. They've seen what Benny sees. The illness that covers the group of men. They know this is as close as they dare go.

'What's He doing?' whispers Sarah. 'Why is Jesus sending them away? That's not what He usually does. When people need Him, He doesn't send them away.'

Benny doesn't take his eyes from Jesus, or from the group of men who do as they're told to do, and walk away in search of a priest. He glances from one to the other and back again.

Something is going to happen … Something has *got* to happen …

On the outskirts of the village, one of the men suddenly stops walking. He points, astonished, at the man next to him – who points right back at him.

The ten men all turn to look at each other. They stare in amazement. They start to laugh.

They lift their hands to touch their faces; pull up their sleeves to look at the skin on their arms. They lift their tunics to peer at the skin on their feet, their legs. Skin that is smooth and clear. Skin that shows no trace of any disease!

Skin that is completely better.

And they gasp for breath. They suck in air by the lungful as they try to grasp the truth: they're not sick anymore. They're healed!

They had cried out to Jesus and He gave them back their health – which means He's given them back their lives.

All they can do is laugh and cry and hug each other, and run away to find their families. To tell them – to *show* them – the breathtaking news!

At least, all but one man runs away. A man who isn't a Jew.

A man who's from Samaria.

When he sees his clear, smooth skin, when he touches his soft, warm face, he twists around. He gazes back towards Jesus, to where he has left Him standing a short way from the village.

And he runs.

He runs, shouting praises to God, all the way back to Jesus and he throws himself in the dirt at His Healer's feet.

His Saviour's feet.

'Thank You!' Over and over again he sobs: 'Thank You, Lord, thank You!'

Jesus' eyes smile as they look at him. Deep and kind. They glow with love for this man who is better.

Then, 'There were ten of you, weren't there?' Jesus says. His voice sounds full and rich to the man who still kneels on the ground. 'There were ten of you who were ill, and ten of you who have been made well again. So **WHERE ARE THE OTHER NINE?** Why is it only you, the man from Samaria, who has come back to say thank You to God?'

The man says nothing. What can he say?

Jesus smiles at him again.

'Up you get,' He says. 'And off you go. Your faith has made you well.'

Topz see the man get to his feet. He doesn't look small and fragile anymore. He stands straight and tall, like Jesus.

And they watch as he walks away, to find his family, to find his friends – with a spring in every single step.

CHAPTER 15

Because He's Promised

(Luke 18:1–8)

Topz lie flat out on their backs on the ground in a long line. Paul is at the head. Then Josie, who lies with the top of her head just touching the soles of his sandals, feet pointing in the same direction as his. Then Danny, whose head touches *her* sandals, then Dave, Sarah, Benny, all lying in the same way, with John at the end of the line.

'Everyone in position?' asks Paul.

'Yup,' says Benny. 'Now what?'

'Now,' answers Paul, 'I make a mark with my head.' As he speaks, he wriggles his head about in the dust. 'And whoever's at the end, make a mark with your feet. As deep as you can.'

'That's me,' calls John.

'Are you doing it?' Paul calls back.

John digs his heels into the dirt; scrapes them from side to side. 'Done it.'

'Cool,' says Paul. 'We can get up now.'

John rolls to one side and scrambles to his feet with the others.

Paul walks all the way down from his head mark to John's feet mark.

'That is long,' he grins. 'That is *really* tall! That is how tall someone would be if they were as tall as all of us put together.'

'It's not very likely, though, is it?' says Benny. 'To find someone that tall.'

'Maybe not,' nods Paul. 'But then, who knows? There might be some undiscovered island somewhere where being as tall as this is normal. Where being our size might actually be thought of as *really* weird and tiny.'

'You *are* a bit weird, Paul,' says Sarah. 'And I don't mean that in a nasty way,' she adds quickly. 'If you weren't weird, you wouldn't be Paul.'

'Anyway, weird is good,' says Josie. 'After all, how many people are there who would think of lying on the ground to see how tall a person they could make? Not many, I'll bet.'

Paul's eyes twinkle. He puts a hand to his head to brush the dust from his hair. A fine cloud of dirt puffs out.

'You might want to have a swim later,' grins Dave. 'Your hair looks a bit – well – clogged.'

'Does it?' answers Paul. He rubs his hands a little harder against his head. 'It's these curls. Stuff gets trapped in them.'

Benny raises his eyebrows. 'Stuff like what?'

'Oh, you know – stuff. I found a bit of cheese once.'

'A bit of cheese?' Sarah wrinkles her nose. 'How on earth did a bit of cheese get caught in your hair?'

'No idea,' Paul says, 'but it was quite handy when it happened 'cos I was feeling really peckish.'

Topz stop walking, disbelieving eyes fixed on their curly-haired friend.

He turns; looks back at them. 'What?'

As they reach the edge of the village where Jesus is staying, they see Him with His disciples. His friends have joined Him on His journey to Jerusalem.

But Jesus doesn't rest.

This isn't a moment for Him to relax and be quiet. It isn't even a moment for Him to speak with God.

It's a time for Him to teach His disciples something more. Another opportunity to help their relationship with God to grow.

'Jesus never wastes time, does He?' says Josie. 'If there's a moment to seize for God, He always seizes it.'

'I have a story for you,' Jesus says. 'There was once a judge. He wasn't afraid of God and he certainly didn't respect people. But he was troubled by a widow. A widow who just wouldn't leave him alone.

'Now this widow,' Jesus continues, 'kept on going to him to plead for her rights. She wouldn't let the matter drop. "Please!" she cried, over and over again.

"Please, I'm asking you to help me. I'm begging you to see that justice is done!"

'The judge tried to ignore her. He didn't care about her. Her troubles weren't his troubles, and for a long time he turned his back on her. He wouldn't lift a finger to help.

'But,' Jesus says, 'there finally came a time when he couldn't stand it any longer. He thought to himself, "Hmm ... I'm not afraid of God and I certainly don't respect people. But this widow is giving me so much trouble by going on and on and *on* that I will make sure the right thing happens for her. If I don't, she'll wear me to a frazzle because she'll never leave me alone – as sure as I'm a judge!"'

Jesus looks around at His friends' faces. They listen intently; watch Him with keen, bright eyes.

But have they understood His story?

'What do you think about that dreadful judge?' He asks. 'He couldn't be more different to God, could he? God, who loves every single person so much. Who wants to be a part of your lives. Who simply can't get enough of each one of you!

'When you cry out to God day in and day out, night after night – won't He listen to you? Won't He make sure that the right thing happens for you? Of course He will!'

Again Jesus studies the faces that gaze at Him.

'You can rely on God,' He says. 'You can trust in Him completely. Totally. But let me ask you this. When the Son of Man comes back, will He find faith on the earth?'

Clouds are building in the sky overhead. They rise up from the horizon; a mass of pale grey that drifts across the blue until it shuts out the sun.

'Jesus is telling us never to stop talking to God,' Josie says. 'That's right, isn't it? That's what He means. We mustn't ever give up. If a mean judge does the right thing for someone just because they keep on at him and he wants to shut them up, then God will want to do so much more for us. Because He loves us and He never wants to stop hearing from us.'

Danny watches the sky. He feels the cooler air against his face as the sun is blotted out by the bank of cloud. Somewhere inside him, he's uneasy.

'He said it again, though,' he murmurs. 'Jesus said again about coming back.'

'Because He will,' answers Sarah. 'And when He does, **HE WANTS US TO BE READY FOR HIM**. That's why He doesn't waste a moment. There aren't any moments to waste! People need to know that they can trust God. That they can talk to God and He'll listen. That God will never let them down. Because …'

She stops. She takes a deep breath. 'Because there'll be a time when Jesus isn't here. When He isn't physically with us. And we'll never know how long it'll be before He comes back again. We just know that He will.'

Josie glances at her friend. She feels the tears spring to her eyes and she can't blink them away.

Sarah gives her hand a squeeze. '**JESUS WILL COME BACK**, Josie,' she says. 'Because He promised.'

CHAPTER 16
Noses Aren't for Looking Down
(Luke 18:9–14)

The sky stays grey and full of cloud. The air is still. It feels thick and heavy.

'Maybe we're in for a storm,' says John.

He peers towards the horizon and shivers. He's not cold but a shudder still shakes him. 'I don't like storms,' he grunts.

Topz wait for Jesus to move: to go back to the village or to head off once more for Jerusalem.

He doesn't. He stays where He is and talks with His disciples.

Other people start to join them. Like Topz, as soon as they see Jesus, they want to stay close to Him. They want to hear Him speak.

Jesus doesn't keep them waiting long.

'There's something you must be very careful *not* to do,' He begins. 'And that is to look down your nose at anyone. I'm going to tell you the story of two men. One man was a Pharisee, and one was a tax collector, and they both went to the Temple to talk to God.'

Jesus goes on, 'Let's look at what the Pharisee did first. He found a space by himself and he said to God, "Thank You, God, that I am not greedy and don't do dishonest and wrong things. Thank you that I am not a bad person like all the others."

'The Pharisee glanced over at the tax collector. "Oh, thank You, God, that I am not like him!" he gloated. "Yes, that thief of a tax collector over there! No, God, I fast for two days every week. It's true, not a crumb of food passes my lips in that time. Not only that, but I give You one tenth of everything I earn."

'Now,' Jesus says, 'let's see what the tax collector did. Well, the tax collector kept his distance from the Pharisee. He wouldn't even look at him, let alone lift his face towards God. He was too ashamed. No, with his head down and thumping on his own chest to show how upset he was, he cried out to God, "Dear Lord, please take pity on me. I am a man who has done so many things wrong!"

'Let me tell you,' Jesus continues, 'it was not the Pharisee who had put himself right with God when he left the Temple and went home. It was the tax collector. You see, my friends, people who think that they are better than others – who try to make themselves big and important – God will bring them down. But those who are humble – those who know that they need God's help and forgiveness – those are the people who God will lift up, who He will make great. Those are the people who will be with Him forever.'

Josie scrambles to her feet. 'I'm going for a walk.'

Without waiting for anyone to answer, she starts to

march quickly away from the rest of the Gang, from Jesus and the growing crowd of listeners.

Sarah blinks after her in surprise. 'Do you want me to come with you?' she calls.

Her friend waves a hand behind her. 'No, it's fine. Thanks, but I'll be okay.'

'Well, how long will you be?'

Josie turns briefly, her shoulders hunched in a shrug. Then she carries on walking.

Are You there, God?

Her voice sounds so small. Josie speaks the words out into the stillness as she slips off by herself, but they seem to her to get lost somewhere in the muggy air. Snatched away by the vastness of the plains into the wide expanse of grey over her head.

Into the hugeness of God's creation.

No, silly question. I KNOW You're there, because that's Your promise. But sometimes ... I still feel all alone. So small and so unimportant. When I look at everything You've created – it's enormous! Even here, this one place where Jesus is. Even if this was the only place that existed in the whole universe – it's still so big!

And who am I, God? So, so tiny in the middle of it all. How is it possible that You can even see me? Or care about me?

But I know You do love me.

Jesus says that You will always hear us. You will always answer us. Not because we keep on and on at You and You want us to be quiet, but because of how much You love us. Even if Your answer is 'no' to something, 'no' is still an answer. And if You do answer 'no' it's because it's not right. It's because You can see more than we can ever see. You see everything! You know what's best for us in a way that we can never understand because we only see a snatch of what's going on. But You have the whole, complete picture.

Which is why we have to trust You.

Which is why I want to trust You.

Please help me, God, to be more the person You want me to be. I want to be with You forever, God. In all my tinyness. I know I do wrong things and I'm sorry. I want to be like the tax collector in Jesus' story. **I NEVER WANT TO FORGET HOW MUCH I NEED YOU.** How much I need Your forgiveness.

And I never want to look at other people and think that I'm better than they are or that I would never do the wrong things that they do. Because we all do things You don't like, things that make You sad. And we all need to say sorry. Please help me, God, never to look down my nose at someone else.

So, yes, I know You're there. I know You'll always be there. But right now – right this minute in this huge space – I feel all alone. I feel so sad.

You see, I don't want Jesus to go away, God.

I know He has to. I know that's what has to happen. And I know that when He goes, He'll be with You. He'll be right next to You where He belongs.

And I know we'll still be able to talk to Him – exactly the way we talk to You, because Jesus promises that He'll always be with us, too. It's because of Jesus that we can talk to You at all!

But something horrible is going to happen.

Jesus still has to leave the earth. One day, He'll come back, but for now He still has to leave. He still has to go away.

And I don't want Him to ...

CHAPTER 17
Like a Child
(Luke 18:15–17)

Gruff races off through the trees. All of a sudden.

John yells. 'Gruff! Gruff, come back! Come here
– NOW!'

He pelts after him. He leaps over a rock, then trips on
a tree root and tumbles to the ground.

'Ugh!' he grunts.

As he rolls over onto his back, suddenly Gruff's
face is there, right above his. The dog pushes his nose
towards John's nose. His tail wags furiously and his
bright eyes seem to ask, 'What's going on? Why are
you lying down?'

'You see, Gruff,' says John, pushing himself up to lean
on his elbows. 'This is your fault. If you hadn't run off,
I wouldn't have had to chase after you. And if I hadn't
chased after you, I wouldn't be flat out in the dirt.'

Gruff continues to stare at him. His tail carries on
beating the air.

It's only after another moment that John spots it.

His dog holds something in his mouth.

John frowns. 'What's that? What have you got there?'

He reaches out a hand, but as quick as lightning, Gruff leaps out of the way. John tries again to catch hold of whatever he's found, but once more, Gruff is too quick for him.

'Fine,' John sighs. 'You wanna play? Let's play.'

He gets to his feet. Gruff springs excitedly around him and John gets ready to play chase.

That's when he hears it. A child crying. A very small child.

John peers through the trees. There's nothing to see. No one there.

Gruff nudges his legs impatiently.

'Ssh, Gruff, down!' John hisses.

Then he hears a voice. It's faint. It must be a little distance away.

'Don't worry,' the voice says. 'We'll find it, you'll see. Let's go and look.'

Again Gruff nudges at John. He jumps up to place his front paws on his owner's legs.

John leans down; narrows his eyes to try to see what it is Gruff holds in his mouth. He still can't make it out. Except that it looks like wood.

Someone laughs.

John straightens up.

'You see?' says the boy who's just stepped out from among the trees. 'If a dog's going to run off with one of your toys, you couldn't pick a friendlier one than Gruff.'

John's face breaks into a broad grin. 'Isaac! What are you doing here?'

'Visiting family,' smiles Isaac. 'This is my little cousin, Anna. Anna, meet my friend, John. Oh, and Gruff, of course.'

Gruff instantly bounds towards him, tail wagging even more frantically than it was before.

The little girl who stands next to him holding tightly onto his hand has stopped crying. She doesn't look at John. Her face scrunches itself into a frown as she studies Gruff. Then she points with her free hand.

'Donkey! My donkey!'

John gives a short laugh. 'No!' he grins. 'Gruff's not a donkey. Like Isaac says, he's a dog.'

It's Isaac's turn to laugh. 'Well, of course Gruff's a dog,' he chuckles. 'But if you look in his mouth, you'll find there's a donkey.'

Before John has time to have another good peer into Gruff's face, Isaac has commanded, 'Sit!'

Gruff sits.

'Now, drop!' says Isaac.

Gruff watches him, tail swishing back and forth in the dust under the trees. But he doesn't open his mouth.

'Drop it, Gruff!' Isaac repeats.

And at last, Gruff lets his treasured find fall from his jaws.

In barely a second, Anna scoops it up. Once it's safely in her hands, she scowls at Gruff crossly.

'Bad dog,' she scolds. *'My* donkey. *Mine*!'

'There you are, Anna,' smiles Isaac. 'Told you we'd get it back.'

'Can I see?' asks John.

Anna eyes him distrustfully. As if, should she open her hands, John would snatch the wooden donkey and run off with it, too.

'Go on, show him,' says Isaac.

Reluctantly, Anna does. She keeps a wary eye on Gruff at the same time.

The donkey is carved from a small block of wood. All the details are carefully crafted: ears, eyes, mane, even its nostrils.

John darts a glance towards Isaac. 'You didn't ... did you?'

Isaac nods. 'It's Anna's birthday. I wanted to make her something.'

'You're so clever!' John says. 'Your cousin is so clever, Anna, d'you know that?

That is a stonking donkey! I'd never be able to make anything like that.'

'Yeah, you would,' shrugs Isaac. 'It's just a donkey. I copied ours.'

'Has it got a name?' John asks.

Once again, Anna scowls. 'Of course,' she mumbles.

'D'you want to tell me what it is?'

Anna lets out a deep sigh, as if John and his dog are about the most troublesome things she has ever come across.

'It's Donkey,' she mutters. 'Because he's a donkey.'

Donkey doesn't seem to be any the worse for his adventure in Gruff's mouth. But as the four of them wander on out of the trees back to Anna's village, Anna holds him in both hands tightly, keeping him close to her chest. Just to be on the safe side.

Anna's village isn't very big. But today it's busy. Packed with people. Not just those who live there, visitors, too.

And it doesn't take long to realise why.

Jesus is there. His disciples are with Him. He's been teaching and they've listened to Him, along with the gathering crowd.

In a quiet moment, a family make their way towards Him. A mother and father and two young boys. Behind them, another father carries his little daughter on his shoulders. And behind him is still another mother, and another father, each with their children. Even grandparents are there with small grandchildren who cling to them.

For every adult, the request is the same:

'Please, Jesus, please bless my child … Please bless my children, my grandchildren. Lay Your hands on them, Lord, and bless them.'

When Jesus' disciples see the family groups begin to step forward out of the crowd, to move towards Jesus, they look annoyed.

They start to scold them. 'No, sorry, but you'll have to get back into your places. Can't you see how busy Jesus is? He doesn't have time for this!'

John is surprised. He's never heard Jesus' friends talk like this before. He's never known Jesus to send anyone away.

But then Jesus' voice rings out.

'Don't stop these children coming to see me,' He says to the scolders. 'Don't *ever* stop children coming to meet me! God's kingdom belongs to little children just like these. They are just as welcome to be His friends and to live with Him forever as anyone else! Never forget,' He adds, 'everyone needs to accept who God is the way a little child accepts who their parents are. That's the way to enter God's kingdom. To really *know His love*.'

Anna stands for a moment between Isaac and John. She watches as Jesus talks to the children around Him; as He places a hand on them and blesses them.

She glances up at Isaac.

He smiles at her and gives her a little nod.

And with Donkey still clutched in her hands, she runs forward for her blessing too.

CHAPTER 18

True

(Luke 18:31–34)

Danny runs as fast as he can. Back towards the rock.

There are Topz all over it. They sit, they sprawl; Paul is fast asleep.

'We've got to go!' Danny calls as he races towards them.

Sarah glances over her shoulder. 'Paul's sleeping.'

'Then wake him up!' Danny shouts – not so that Sarah will hear, but so that Paul will open his eyes. 'Come on, they're leaving now!'

Benny groans. 'Can't we just sit here for a little bit longer? I'm worn out. And you *know* what happens when I get worn out,' he adds. 'I get hungry. And you *know* what happens when I get hungry.'

'Yup,' mutters Dave. 'King sized bad mood time.'

'King *and* queen sized bad mood time,' nods Josie.

'King and queen and a whole palace full of royal people sized bad mood time,' agrees John.

'Yeah, all right, all right,' says Benny. 'I'm not that bad. At least I'm not a massive great sleepy head like Paul.'

Benny gives Paul a nudge in the ribs with his elbow.

His friend jolts awake. 'What ...? Sorry ...?' he mumbles.

He blinks, confused. Then, 'Who's got a massive great head?' he asks.

'*You* have,' says Benny. 'And it's always asleep.'

'Can't help it.' Paul rubs his eyes. 'I'm worn out. And you *know* what happens when I get worn out.'

'Yeah, yeah,' chuckles Josie. 'You get hungry. We've done all this.'

'No,' answers Paul. 'I go to sleep.'

Danny can't keep still. He knows Jesus and His disciples are getting ready to leave and he's itching to go after them.

Topz clamber slowly to their feet. They stretch. They brush themselves down.

'Erm ... Any chance you could hurry up a bit?' Danny says.

'We *are* hurrying,' grunts Benny.

A few moments later and Danny can't bear it any longer. 'I'm off,' he says. 'You can catch me up.'

'We'll be ready in a minute,' says Sarah. She stoops to pick up Saucy and tuck her into her bag.

Danny has already started to run again. Back the way he came.

'Where are they going this time?' calls Dave.

'Jericho!' yells Danny, without stopping. 'I think they're heading for Jericho.'

At the far side of the village, Danny sees them. Jesus and His twelve disciples. He hasn't missed them. They walk along together, until, with the streets and houses and people a little behind them, Jesus stops.

Danny slows his pace.

He watches and waits.

'You know where we're going, don't you?' Jesus says to His friends. 'We're going to Jerusalem. And when we're there, everything that has been written about the Son of Man – all that the prophets have said will happen – will come true. The Son of Man will be arrested,' He explains quietly. 'He will be laughed at, made fun of. He'll have insults thrown at Him. He'll be spat at and He'll be beaten.'

He pauses. His eyes cloud over.

'And this will happen, too,' He says. 'He will be killed.'

The disciples glance at each other. They've heard Jesus talk like this before, but what does He mean? They listen – they hear Him – but somehow they can't grasp the meaning of His words.

Jesus speaks again. His voice is stronger now. His eyes clearer.

'But that won't be the end. Remember that, it won't be the end! Because on the third day, *HE WILL COME BACK TO LIFE*.'

As the troop of men moves on, Danny doesn't move with them. He stands still; stares after them. He doesn't understand either. If Jerusalem is such a bad place for Jesus to go, then why is He going?

Why does He have to go?

'Hey, Danny!'

Behind him, Topz are catching up.

'Oh, nice!' says Benny. 'So much for the huge rush.

We're scurrying about like ants 'cos you told us to, and you're just standing around doing nothing!'

Danny shrugs. As his friends reach him, they spot the thirteen men who walk away from them on the road to Jericho.

'Let's go,' says Josie.

They set off, but this time, it's Danny who lags behind.

Josie swivels in the dust. 'You coming, Danny?'

Danny looks at the Gang; looks further into the distance at Jesus. Then, slowly, he walks after them.

CHAPTER 19
Through New Eyes
(Luke 18:35–43)

They are almost there. They've almost reached Jericho.

Dave stops. He shakes his head.

'It's no good, I've got to have a drink of water,' he puffs, reaching for his water flask. 'Don't get me wrong, I love hot days. But this is a *really* hot day. And we've been walking a *really* long time.'

'Nearly there, though,' chirps Josie. Her eyes are bright and clear. She seems excited. 'Nearly in Jericho.'

Benny glances at her. 'Don't you *ever* get tired?'

'Oh, come on, we can't stop now,' she says. 'We can have a rest when we get there.'

The closer they get to the city, the more people appear. Some of them point.

Some start to shout: 'It's Jesus! Look, Jesus is here!' And they turn and run to fetch their families and their friends so that they can come out to see Him, too.

Soon, there are clusters of onlookers lining the road Jesus walks on; big groups and small groups who walk along with Him and His disciples. Sometimes Topz lose sight of Him, as people run in front of them and jostle each other to catch their first glimpse of this Teacher they've heard so much about.

A man who sits by himself on the ground begging goes unnoticed.

Then he speaks: 'What's going on?'

He can't see. He's blind. But he can sense the commotion. He's aware of the swish of tunics as people run along the road. He can hear the jumble of voices, the chatter and laughter. He knows a crowd is gathering. It's growing bigger and bigger, more and more excitable.

But he doesn't know why.

He asks again, calling out. Surely somebody will hear him. Somebody will stop to answer.

'What is it? What's happening?'

A woman throws him a look as she passes. 'It's Jesus!' she cries. 'It's Jesus of Nazareth! He's here – He's walking by here right now!'

The woman doesn't stop; doesn't offer to help the beggar to his feet. She doesn't tell him to be careful in case he should get trodden on accidentally. She hurries on with her friends.

It only takes a second for the begging man to take in what he's been told. Less than a moment for him to grasp that **THIS IS THE GREATEST OPPORTUNITY OF HIS WHOLE LIFE**.

And he *can't* let it slip away from him.

He doesn't know where Jesus is. Has He reached him yet? Has He already passed by? But that doesn't stop him yelling out at the top of his voice: 'Jesus! Jesus, Lord, please hear me! Please take pity on me!'

There are people pushing past him and people who
stand in front of him. They turn and stare at him.
Their faces are filled with disgust. How can this man
dare to call out to Jesus? How can he even dare to draw
attention to himself?

'Sssh!' they hiss at him. 'What do you think you're
doing? Stop making a spectacle of yourself and be quiet!'

But the begging man won't be quiet.

'Jesus!' he yells again, even louder. 'Jesus, please!
Please, Lord, please have pity on me!'

He waits. He listens.

He can't see, but Jesus has stopped walking.
Above the bustle and frenzy, Jesus has heard him.

He casts His eyes across the crowds. He peers through
them in the direction of the voice.

'Bring that man to me,' He says. 'The man who's
calling to me, bring him over here.'

The people nearest to the begging man look
surprised. Does Jesus really want to meet someone like
him? He's so dirty and scruffy. He doesn't look as if he's
washed in weeks.

But Jesus always means what He says, and He
stands waiting.

'Come on, then,' grunts a tall man. 'Let's get you
on your feet.'

With the tall man leading him, the blind beggar slowly,
stiffly, awkwardly makes his way towards Jesus. When he
stands in front of Him, his helper drops back. A hush falls
over the crowd.

'Hello,' smiles Jesus. 'What is it I can do for you?'

The man swallows hard. He's nervous, his mouth so dry.

'Erm ...' he mumbles. 'Sir, please ... I want my sight back. I want to be able to see again.'

Jesus nods His head. 'Then see again, my friend,' He says simply. 'Because of your trust in me, your eyes are all better.'

And all of a sudden, the man's world isn't empty and black anymore. It's dazzlingly, piercingly bright! He throws his hands up to his face to shield his eyes from the light. He blinks and squints and gasps.

Then, as the view in front of him slowly takes shape and focus, he sees the Man who stands there.

The miracle Man, Jesus.

As he gazes at Him, the praises begin to pour from his mouth. Over and over again, he says thank You and the tears of joy stream from his brand-new eyes.

All around him, a clamour and noise builds. People who've seen the miracle, and people who've heard what has happened as the news chases through the crowd, burst out in praise to God.

There are tears on Danny's face, too. And on Sarah's.

'Look what He's done,' Danny murmurs. 'There are people who hate Jesus, but look what He's done!'

'I know,' says Sarah. 'That's what faith can do.'

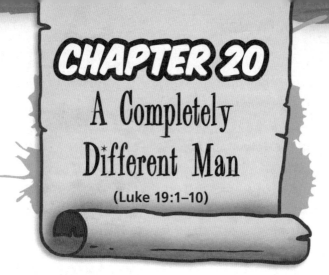

CHAPTER 20
A Completely Different Man
(Luke 19:1–10)

Jericho is buzzing.

Everyone has heard the news, it seems: Jesus has made a blind man see. And Jesus is here somewhere! Now!

The broader city streets are as crammed with people as the narrower alleys of Capernaum village when Jesus is there. There is barely room to move.

'I thought it'd be busy here,' says John. 'But I didn't think it'd be *this* busy.'

He holds Gruff tightly in his arms. He doesn't want to let him run free, he knows he'll lose sight of him.

'No room for a sit down, then,' says Dave.

'Doesn't look like it,' Paul answers. 'Maybe later.'

Dave shakes his head. 'I dunno. Something tells me as long as Jesus is here – it's going to be this busy.'

Topz had lost sight of Jesus ages ago. Before they'd even arrived in Jericho. They'd been swept along the road among the hordes of people who'd turned out to see Him. And where Jesus was by the time they reached the city – how far up ahead of them, or how far behind – they had no idea.

'I can't see a thing,' moans Sarah.

In her bag, Saucy fidgets. She sticks her head out as far as she can, places a paw on Sarah's arm and flexes her claws.

'No, Saucy!' Sarah grumbles. 'You can't come out. If you don't stay in there, I'll lose you. I'll never see you again, ever.'

'Cats, you see,' says John. 'They just haven't got the sense dogs have.'

'Huh,' grunts Sarah. 'And boys haven't got the sense girls have.'

The Gang shuffle on down the street together, squashed by the people on either side of them and bumped by those behind them.

It's not until they round a corner that Josie sees it.

'A tree!' she squeals.

Benny throws her a sideways glance. 'Erm ... yeah, cool, Josie, but in case you haven't realised, we're not actually here to look at trees.'

'I know that!' Josie says. 'But you know what trees are, don't you, Benny?'

Benny frowns. 'Made of ... wood?'

'No! They're *very tall*!'

As she reaches the foot of the tree, Josie quickly scans upwards the full height of the trunk. She sees exactly what she wants to see. If she makes a leap for it, the first branch is just about low enough to grab.

'Stay here,' she hisses to the Gang – and she jumps.

Her hands manage to grasp the lowest branch, but she loses her grip and slips back down to the ground.

'Josie, what are you doing?' says Sarah. 'Why are you doing that now? We're trying to find Jesus.'

'I know,' answers Josie. 'That's why I've got to climb this tree.'

Once again she springs upwards. This time she takes a firm hold of the branch and, pulling on her arms and kicking her legs with a grunt of effort, she is able to hoist herself enough to sit on it.

Paul's face lights up. 'Ha ha!' he chuckles. 'Clever! You'll be able to see for miles up there.'

'I will,' Josie says, clambering to her feet and reaching for the next branch, 'as long as I can get up high enough.'

Topz watch as carefully, nimbly and skilfully, one branch at a time, Josie makes her way towards the crown of the tree. People knock into them, tell them to get out of the way, but they don't move. They press in around the trunk. They need to stay huddled together.

At last, Josie is far enough from the ground to be able to see way over the heads of the crowds beneath her. Holding on as tightly as she can, she narrows her eyes against the sunlight.

She searches one way down the street: people. People everywhere.

But not the Person she's looking for. Not Jesus.

It's the same the other way. Seething, milling crowds. But where is He?

WHERE IS HE?

What Josie sees next is not what she expects to see at all.

A little further down the street is another tree. It's a sycamore tree, like hers, and about the same size. About the same shape. The branches start low on the trunk. It has a broad, spreading crown.

And there – almost at the top, peering through the leaves down to the heads of the people below – is a man.

Like Josie, he has taken advantage of a higher viewpoint.

Like Josie, he looks up and down the street.

And like Josie, she realises, he is looking for Jesus, too.

She can't help laughing. Then her eyes widen.

'There He is!' she murmurs.

The movement in the crowds suddenly seems to slow. Then it stops.

Everyone near the man in the tree appears to turn all together and look up at him – following the gaze of the One everyone has come to see: Jesus.

The man's mouth falls open. Jesus is gazing right at him! And there's a mischievous twinkle in His eye.

Jesus knows exactly who this man is. He's quite famous, but for all the wrong reasons. The man in the tree is the chief tax collector. But it's not just tax that he collects. Like other tax collectors, he grabs and grasps as much money from people as he possibly can, whether it's owed or not. And he uses it to line his own pockets.

Zacchaeus, the man in the tree, is very, very rich. And a thief.

Jesus calls up to him, 'Zacchaeus! How good to see you! Come on down, would you? I need to stay at your house today.'

There's a murmur in the crowd. A murmur of complete surprise, but also of annoyance.

'Doesn't Jesus know who that is?' someone mutters. 'He's a thief! We get poorer and Zacchaeus gets richer!'

Zacchaeus stares. Jesus speaks to him and for a moment, that's all he can do. Just stare.

Then slowly, carefully, he starts to ease himself down

to the ground, slipping from branch to branch, the same way as he climbed up.

When he finally stands in the street next to Jesus, Josie is surprised. Zacchaeus might be a very big thief, but he's also a very tiny man.

'This way, this way,' he ushers Jesus.

He's so amazed at Jesus' request to come to his house, and so delighted to welcome Him that **HIS FACE SHINES**. People move back as much as they can to allow them both to pass.

'There, there!' Josie calls down to her friends, who still wait for her at the foot of her tree.

She points and at last they spot Jesus, too, led by Zacchaeus towards a large house at the corner of the road.

Zacchaeus flings open the door.

'Come in! Come in, Lord!' he cries. And Jesus steps inside.

The people close by can hardly believe their eyes. They frown. They tut.

Someone grumbles, 'We've all turned out to see Jesus, and what's He gone and done? He's invited Himself to the home of a cheat and a thief like Zacchaeus!'

Another voice complains, 'It's a disgrace!'

'They still don't get it, do they?' Josie murmurs. 'Why don't they understand why Jesus is here? It's people like Zacchaeus He's come to help. It's people like Zacchaeus who *need* His help! He's done things wrong but he *knows* he's done things wrong. That's why he looks so excited. He probably thinks Jesus wouldn't want to have anything to do with someone like him.'

Paul looks up at her. 'Are you coming down now?'

She shakes her head. 'Not for a bit. Too busy down there.'

The crowds are still thick. So many wait for Jesus to come outside again; for the chance to see Him and perhaps to hear Him teach. Who knows? He might even ask to come to one of *their* houses.

When the door to the tax collector's house finally opens again, it's not Jesus who comes out first. It's Zacchaeus. He seems half surprised to find the street still packed, and half pleased. He turns to look over his shoulder at Jesus, who steps forward into the sunlight.

'I've decided something, Sir,' Zacchaeus says. His face still shines. His voice trembles with excitement. 'I'm going to give away half of everything I own to the poor. And whoever I have cheated, I will find out the names of each one of them and I will pay them back four times as much as I have stolen!'

No one says a word. The people who watch, the people who listen, stare at him with open mouths and wide eyes.

This is Zacchaeus. This is *Zacchaeus*! But these are the words of a **COMPLETELY DIFFERENT MAN!**

Jesus' face wears the broadest grin. 'You see?' He beams. He speaks to the onlookers. 'This man is an ordinary person, just like you. And today he has been saved! Saved from all the bad things he has done. Saved to live with God forever.'

He faces the crowd, the watchers who still can scarcely believe their ears.

'Do you understand now?' Jesus says. 'This is why I have come! To find those people who are lost. To find them and to save them. What a good day this has been!'

Up high above the ground, her cheek pressed against the trunk of the tree, Josie sees the light in Jesus' eyes as He talks. She sees the love and the warmth in Zacchaeus' face as he looks at the people around him, tells them he's sorry; shakes hands with them.

Zacchaeus stands outside his house in Jericho for the first time as a brand-new person.

And in her head and in her heart, Josie whispers, 'I'll follow You wherever You go, Lord Jesus. All the way to Jerusalem. I will ... *I'll follow You to the very end.*'

Colourful daily Bible reading notes just for you

In each issue the Topz Gang teach you biblical truths through word games, puzzles, riddles, cartoons, competitions, simple prayers and daily Bible readings.

Available as an annual subscription or as single issues.

For current prices or to purchase go to **www.cwr.org.uk/store** call 01252 784700 or visit a Christian bookshop.